MATTHEW

A SELF-STUDY GUIDE

Irving L. Jensen

MOODY PRESS
CHICAGO

ISBN: 0-8024-4459-8

5 7 9 10 8 6

Printed in the United States of America

Contents

Introduction

The Person of Jesus Christ is the key to all history, its grand miracle. One of the keenest Christian writers of the nineteenth century gave this testimony:

> The Person of Christ is to me the surest as well as the most sacred of all facts; as certain as my own personal existence; yea, even more so: for Christ lives in me, and he is the only valuable part of my existence. I am nothing without my Saviour; I am all with him, and would not exchange him for the whole world.[1]

Who is Jesus, and what did He do while on earth to make all history revolve around Him? Is He the Messiah—the Christ—foretold in the Old Testament? Is He really the King of kings and Lord of lords? Answers to these and similar questions are to be found in Matthew's gospel. If you are a Christian, your study in this gospel will deepen your knowledge of Christ and bring you into a more intimate relationship with Him.

Suggestions for Study

1. The key to fruitful Bible study is *you*. The Holy Spirit is your Teacher, but He ministers in proportion to how you apply yourself in study and seek His instruction, in faith.

2. Regard the Bible as a mirror. As you read the Bible, let the Bible read you.

3. Be very conscious of words and short phrases as you analyze the Bible text. If you are meeting in a Bible study group, concentrate most of your discussion on these words and phrases. This will help keep your group study Bible-based.

1. Philip Schaff, *The Person of Christ* (New York: Amer. Tract Soc., 1880), p. 5.

4. It is important to have an edition of the Bible that has read-able, clear print, and space in the margins for notations. Mark your Bible freely as you study (for example, underline key words and phrases). You will be surprised how this will aid your study.

5. Use a notebook or single sheets of paper for recording your studies as you proceed. This manual will suggest things to re-cord in each lesson.

6. Read Matthew 28:20. Let these words of Jesus be an inspira-tion and challenge to you throughout your study of this gospel.

ACKNOWLEDGMENT

The author wishes to recognize artist Henry Franz for his work in drawing the charts and maps for all the books of this self-study series.

Lesson 1
Background of Matthew

The background of the writing of Matthew's gospel provides a good introduction to its message. Here is where motivations to study are stirred and specific goals laid out.

There are four main stages in the study of a book of the Bible. These stages are:

1. Learning the *background* of the book (e.g., for whom was it originally written?)

2. Making a *survey* of the book as a whole

3. Making a firsthand *analysis* of each part (e.g., chapter) of the book (observation, interpretation, application)

4. Referring to outside helps (e.g., commentaries) for supplementary and checking aid

Background, the first stage of study, is the subject of this lesson. Lesson 2 is devoted to the second stage, survey, and the remaining lessons are the core of your study of Matthew, which is analysis of the Bible text.

I. AUTHOR AND TITLE

As with the other three gospels, authorship of this first gospel account is not identified by name. Tradition is unanimous in ascribing the writing to Matthew, son of Alphaeus, whose Jewish name was Levi. Matthew was the publican (tax collector) whom Jesus called to be His disciple. Read Matthew 9:9-13.

Read these other New Testament verses, which are our only source of information about the man Matthew: Matt. 10:3; Mark 2:14-17; 3:18; Luke 5:27-32; Acts 1:13.

The title assigned to this gospel by the early church was "The Gospel According to Matthew." The word "gospel" means "good

6

news." Why, then, are the words "according to" more accurate than "of"?

II. ORIGINAL READERS

It is clear from the content of this Bible book that it was written for the immediate audience of Jews. Since the first hearers of the spoken gospel were mainly Jews, it does not surprise us that one of the four gospels was directed especially to them, answering questions uppermost in their minds about Jesus, such as

Was Jesus truly descended from David?

What was Jesus' attitude toward the Old Testament law?

Did He come to establish the kingdom promised in the Old Testament?

This is why Matthew was the most highly valued and widely read of the four gospels in the first decades of the early church.

This gospel is not exclusively Jewish, however. Throughout the account, Jesus' ministry is related to all the people of the world, such as in the Great Commission of 28:19-20 and in Jesus' identification of Himself as the Son of man (e.g., 16:13).[1]

III. DATE AND PLACE WRITTEN

A possible date for the writing of Matthew is A.D. 58. This was before the destruction of Jerusalem (A.D. 70) and shortly before Luke wrote his account (see Appendix). There is strong reason to believe that Matthew was the first of the four gospels to be written.

Matthew may have written this gospel from Jerusalem or Antioch of Syria. The history of the manuscript's circulation from place to place, and of copies made from it, is not known to us today. "Each of the four Gospels, with its distinctive picture of Christ, seems to have circulated at first in the churches of a particular area, but shortly after the appearance of the fourth the four appear to have been bound up together and acknowledged by the churches at large as the authoritative fourfold Gospel of Christ."[2]

IV. PURPOSE AND THEME

Matthew's gospel is the historical connecting link between the Old and New Testaments. This is shown on Chart A. Matthew is

---

1. The book of Acts clearly shows that the first Christians were mainly of Jewish stock and that eventually the fellowship was enlarged by the extension of a ministry to Gentiles.
2. F. F. Bruce, *The Books and the Parchments* (Westwood, N.J.: Revell, 1963), p. 93.

preeminently the gospel of fulfillment. The writer seeks "to connect the memories of his readers with their hopes; to show that the Lord of the Christian was the Messiah of the Jew," the King of the promised kingdom.[3]

MATTHEW'S LOCATION IN THE BIBLE

Chart A

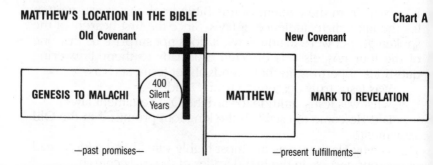

Of the thirty sections in Matthew that are peculiar to that gospel, most have a bearing on the theme of Christ as King. Read Acts 1:3-6 and observe that the subject of Christ's kingdom was prominent on Jesus' lips and in the inquiring hearts of the disciples just before Jesus ascended to heaven.

Listed below are major subjects appearing throughout this gospel that would be of special interest to Jews with Old Testament background. Read the verses cited.

"holy city"; "holy place"—4:5; 24:15; 27:53

"son of David"—1:1, 20; 9:27; 12:23; 15:22; 20:30-31; 21:9, 15, 22:42, 45

fulfillment of Old Testament prophecy—1:22; 2:5, 15, 17, 23; 4:14; 8:17; 12:17; 13:35; 21:4, 42; 26:31, 54, 56; 27:9-10

Jewish customs—15:1-2; 27:62

law of Moses—5:17-19, 21, 27, 31, 33, 38, 43; 7:12; 11:13; 12:5; 15:6; 22:36, 40; 23:23

"kingdom of heaven"—(more than 30 references: consult a concordance)

Old Testament prophets—(39 references)

The above selections illustrate the classic couplet:

> The New Testament is in the Old concealed;
> The Old Testament is in the New revealed.

Of this, Joseph Parker writes:

> Even in Genesis the leaves are stirring; the air blows upon us from another world. You feel that someone is coming, and so all through the Old Testament. Now it is a sudden flash of light,

3. See W. Graham Scroggie, *Know Your Bible*, 2:37.

LIFE OF CHRIST SHOWING COVERAGE BY MATTHEW (shaded area)

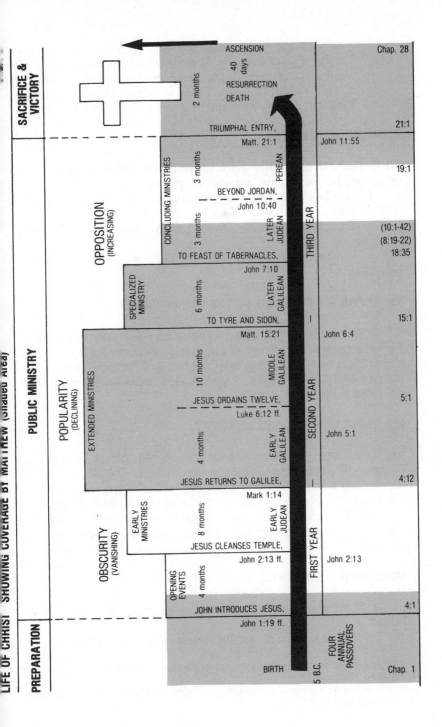

PREPARATION	PUBLIC MINISTRY			SACRIFICE & VICTORY

PREPARATION

JOHN INTRODUCES JESUS,
John 1:19 ff.

BIRTH
5 B.C.
FOUR ANNUAL PASSOVERS
Chap. 1
4:1

PUBLIC MINISTRY

OBSCURITY (VANISHING)

OPENING EVENTS — 4 months — EARLY JUDEAN

JESUS CLEANSES TEMPLE,
John 2:13 ff.
John 2:13

EARLY MINISTRIES — 8 months — EARLY JUDEAN

JESUS RETURNS TO GALILEE,
Mark 1:14
4:12

POPULARITY (DECLINING)

EXTENDED MINISTRIES

— 4 months — EARLY GALILEAN

JESUS ORDAINS TWELVE,
Luke 6:12 ff.
John 5:1
5:1

— 10 months — MIDDLE GALILEAN

TO TYRE AND SIDON,
Matt. 15:21
John 6:4
15:1

SPECIALIZED MINISTRY — 6 months — LATER GALILEAN

TO FEAST OF TABERNACLES,
John 7:10
18:35
(8:19-22)
(10:1-42)

OPPOSITION (INCREASING)

CONCLUDING MINISTRIES

— 3 months — LATER JUDEAN

BEYOND JORDAN,
John 10:40

— 3 months — PEREAN

TRIUMPHAL ENTRY,
Matt. 21:1
John 11:55
19:1
21:1

FIRST YEAR   SECOND YEAR   THIRD YEAR

SACRIFICE & VICTORY

ASCENSION
40 days
RESURRECTION
DEATH
— 2 months —

Chap. 28
21:1

9

now a transparent darkness. We feel it in history, in psalms, in prophecy. Sometimes a great voice of thunder, sometimes a still, small voice of comfort. Did I hear the blast of a trumpet miles and miles away, rising and falling in cadence? It is the sign of the King's approach. There will be a new personality amongst us.[4]

V. PROMINENT FEATURES

Three features especially characterize this gospel written in a style described by the words "antique simplicity":

    1. Five key discourses of Jesus (of the gospel's 1071 verses, 644 contain spoken words of Jesus)

    2. Great Jewish themes: about Law, Messiah, Prophecy, Kingdom, Israel

    3. Many references to the fulfillment of Old Testament prophecy.

VI. MATTHEW'S COVERAGE OF THE LIFE OF CHRIST

When all four gospels are harmonized into one story of the life of Christ, a composite picture of His earthly ministry appears. This is shown on Chart B. Each gospel reports only selected events and discourses of Jesus' career.[5] The shaded areas on Chart B show how much is reported by Matthew.

VII. GEOGRAPHY OF JESUS' MINISTRY

The main ingredients of history are people, places, things, and events—all prominent in the gospel account. The second ingredient, places, is the subject of geography. Study the map until you are familiar with the places where Jesus ministered. Observe on the survey Chart D the regions of Jesus' ministry covered by Matthew. Visualize all geographical places whenever they appear in the Matthew account. This will be of great help in your study.

SOME REVIEW QUESTIONS

    1. What are the four main stages of study of a book of the Bible?

    2. What is known about the author of the first gospel?

4. Quoted in W. W. White, *Thirty Studies in the Gospel by Matthew* (privately published, 1902), p. 12.
5. In fact, the four gospels together report only a small part of Jesus' total ministry (see John 21:25).

3. Who were the intended original readers of Matthew? What evidences in the book itself point to this?

4. When and where did Matthew write the gospel?

5. What is the main theme of this gospel? How is it related to the Old Testament? Why do you think it was placed first in the New Testament canon?

6. What are some of the prominent features of Matthew's gospel?

7. Who should read and study Matthew in this twentieth century? How do its prophecies (fulfilled and yet to be fulfilled) make it relevant to the world of today?

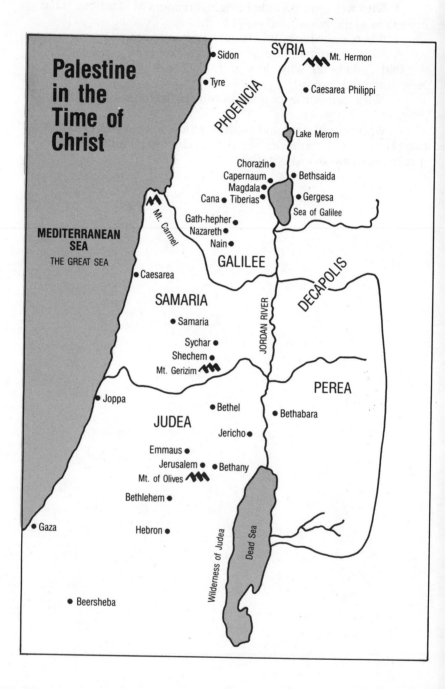

Palestine in the Time of Christ

SYRIA

Sidon

Tyre

PHOENICIA

Mt. Hermon

Caesarea Philippi

Lake Merom

Chorazin

Capernaum

Magdala

Cana • Tiberias

Bethsaida

Gergesa

Sea of Galilee

Mt. Carmel

Gath-hepher

Nazareth

Nain

GALILEE

MEDITERRANEAN SEA

THE GREAT SEA

Caesarea

SAMARIA

Samaria

Sychar

Shechem

Mt. Gerizim

JORDAN RIVER

DECAPOLIS

PEREA

Joppa

Bethel

JUDEA

Jericho

Emmaus

Jerusalem • Bethany

Mt. of Olives

Bethlehem

Gaza

Hebron

Bethabara

Wilderness of Judea

Dead Sea

Beersheba

Lesson 2
Survey of Matthew

Now that we are ready to study the actual text of Matthew's gospel, where should we begin? The answer is, begin with the large whole, and then move on to the smaller parts. The large, overall view is known by various names: skyscraper view, bird's-eye view, overview, survey. The detailed study of the small parts is called analysis.

In Lesson 1 we studied the background of Matthew's gospel in order to appreciate *how* and *why* it was given to the world. Now as we enter the stage of survey study, followed by analysis in subsequent lessons, our goal is to learn *what* the gospel says and means.

I. PREPARING TO SURVEY

Open your Bible to Matthew and rapidly turn the pages of its twenty-eight chapters. As you do this, prepare your mind to get a general overview of this book, just as a tourist would view New York City from the top of the Empire State Building. This is what survey study is all about—seeing the layout of the book as a whole and getting the "feel" of its contents. Survey study should always precede analysis.[1] The rule is "Image the whole; then execute the parts." (Have you ever tried thumbing through a magazine first for a casual acquaintance and then returning to read the individual articles and features?)

Use a Bible in which you will not hesitate to make pencil notations. Throughout your study, whether survey or analysis, always keep a pencil in hand as your read the Bible text, and use it to record your observations.

1. The survey and analytical methods of study are treated in detail in Irving L. Jensen, *Independent Bible Study*.

II. FIRST READING

Your first reading of Matthew should be a mere scanning. Spend an hour to an hour and a half (averaging two to three minutes per chapter) viewing only the prominent features of each chapter.[2] Don't try to be exhaustive in this stage of study. The main purpose of this scanning is to make a first acquaintance by identifying things that stand out.

CHAPTER TITLES **Chart C**

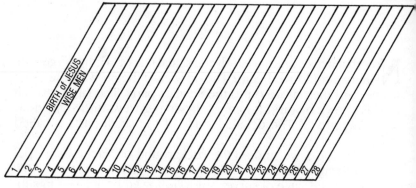

After you have scanned each chapter, record on Chart C chapter titles similar to the titles shown. (A chapter title is a strong word or phrase, preferably taken from the text, intended to serve as a clue to at least one main part of the chapter. The sum total of chapter titles is *not* intended to be a comprehensive outline of contents.)

Other things to look for in this scanning are:

main characters	main events
various groups	discourses of Jesus
opposition to Jesus	

What are some of your impressions of Matthew's gospel after this first reading?

III. SECOND READING

As you browse through the gospel a second time, keep in mind the chapter titles you recorded earlier. Observe key words and

2. The original Bible autographs did not have chapter divisions, or, for that matter, paragraph and verse divisions. Such divisions are helps to us today for reference and for identification of small units of thought.

MATTHEW JESUS AND HIS PROMISED KINGDOM

Chart D

MATTHEW CONTAINS:
15 parables
20 miracles

KEY VERSES: 1:1 "The book of the generation of Jesus Christ, the son of David, the son of Abraham."

2:2 "Where is he that is born King of the Jews? for we have seen his star in the east, and are come to worship him."

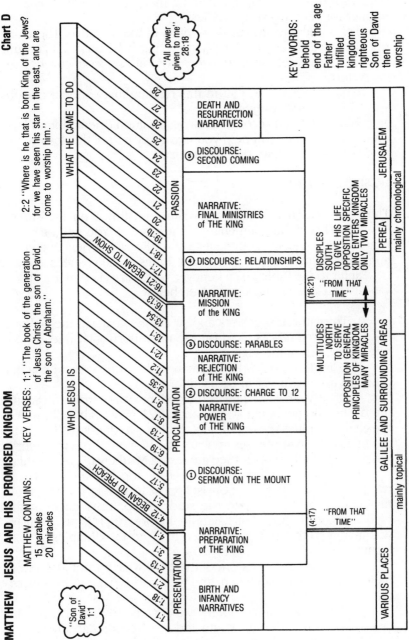

"Son of David" 1:1

WHO JESUS IS

WHAT HE CAME TO DO

"All power given to me" 28:18

KEY WORDS:
behold
end of the age
Father
fulfilled
kingdom
righteous
Son of David
then
worship

PRESENTATION

BIRTH AND INFANCY NARRATIVES

NARRATIVE: PREPARATION of THE KING

4:12 BEGAN TO PREACH

PROCLAMATION

① DISCOURSE: SERMON ON THE MOUNT

NARRATIVE: POWER of THE KING

② DISCOURSE: CHARGE TO 12

NARRATIVE: REJECTION of THE KING

③ DISCOURSE: PARABLES

16:21 BEGAN TO SHOW

NARRATIVE: MISSION of the KING

④ DISCOURSE: RELATIONSHIPS

PASSION

NARRATIVE: FINAL MINISTRIES of THE KING

⑤ DISCOURSE: SECOND COMING

DEATH AND RESURRECTION NARRATIVES

(4:17) "FROM THAT TIME"

(16:21) "FROM THAT TIME"

MULTITUDES
NORTH
TO SERVE
OPPOSITION GENERAL
PRINCIPLES OF KINGDOM
MANY MIRACLES

DISCIPLES
SOUTH
TO GIVE HIS LIFE
OPPOSITION SPECIFIC
KING ENTERS KINGDOM
ONLY TWO MIRACLES

VARIOUS PLACES

GALILEE AND SURROUNDING AREAS

PEREA

JERUSALEM

mainly topical

mainly chronological

1:1 1:18 2:1 2:13 3:1 4:1 5:1 5:17 6:1 6:19 7:13 8:1 9:1 9:35 11:2 12:1 13:1 13:54 16:13 16:21 17:1 18:1 19:1b 20 21 22 23 24 25 26 27 28

15

phrases in this reading, underlining them in your Bible as a reminder for later analytical studies.

Try to identify any turning points in the narrative. These are not always easily detected in Matthew, partly because the account up to Passion Week (chap.16) does not follow a strict chronological pattern.

What stands out to you in this reading that you had not observed in the first reading?

These first and second readings are good orientation to Matthew's gospel; they will help you in the key part of this lesson, the study of a survey chart, discussed next.

IV. SURVEY CHART

The organization of Matthew's writing is shown on the survey Chart D. This is the main chart of the manual. You will be referring to it often during your analytical studies, for review of context and as a reminder of the prominent things of the gospel account.

Refer to the Bible text whenever verses are cited in the observations and study suggestions given below.

1. Thirty-three segments appear on the chart, in the oblique spaces. The references cited on the main horizontal line are the opening verses of the segments.

2. Complete a record of segment titles. (Most of your chapter titles, secured earlier, can be used for this.)

3. Observe that Matthew is divided into three major divisions, the driving points being at 4:12 and 16:21. What Bible phrase on the chart identifies the opening of the last two divisions? Note that the first of the two phrases appears at 4:17, not 4:12. Why, then, is the division made at 4:12? (See the text of Matthew to answer this.)

4. A two-part outline is shown at the top of the chart. These two phases of the gospel of Christ appear in all four gospels, most prominently in Mark. Note the study of contrasts made at the pivotal point of 16:21. For example, before 16:21, Jesus' ministry was mainly to the multitudes: after 16:21, to the disciples; and so forth.

5. Observe at the bottom of the chart what part of Matthew is mainly topical in arrangement and what part is mainly chronological.

6. Note how many chapters are devoted to the birth and infancy narratives and to the death and resurrection narratives.

7. In between the two narrative sections noted above is a series of five discourses, each discourse being introduced by a narrative section. Study this alternating arrangement on the chart

16

carefully. It represents the core of Matthew's gospel. Note the subjects of the five numbered discourses and the outline about Jesus as King in the narrative sections.

8. Observe that the book opens with a reference to Jesus' kingship ("Son of David," 1:1) and closes on the same note ("all power is given to me," 28:18).

9. The title and key verses reflect this theme of Jesus as King.

10. Study the list of key words. As you proceed with your analytical studies, add other key words.

SOME REVIEW QUESTIONS

1. What is the main purpose of survey study?

2. What is the subject of each of the three main divisions of Matthew? What phrases introduce the second and third divisions?

3. What are the subjects of the five great discourses of Jesus as recorded by Matthew?

4. How many key words of Matthew can you remember?

5. Which part of Matthew does not follow a strict chronological pattern?

6. Assign a title to this first gospel account.

As you conclude this study, think of some spiritual lessons that may be learned from the highlights of Matthew's gospel.

Birth and Infancy of the King

If the Old Testament were our only Scripture today, there would be no gospel of Christ, only question marks. Everything about the Old Testament points to the New, so that when we read the opening chapters of this "link" book, Matthew, it is clear that "the coming of Jesus was no afterthought, no isolated event, but rather the actual realization in history of the age-long plan and purpose of God."[1] (Read Gal. 4:4).

This lesson is about Jesus' birth and experiences as an infant. Most people agree that the Christmas story is beautiful, but many do not see the awesome significance of Christ's birth. He was born to die, so that He could save people from their sins. That is one of the great truths recorded in the opening lines of Matthew.

I. PREPARATION FOR STUDY

The best preparation for studying these two chapters is to read the Old Testament setting, including promises and prophecies, which pointed forward to the birth of Jesus. The prophecies whose fulfillments are reported in Matthew 1-2 are included in the preliminary exercises below.

1. The last of Old Testament recorded history and prophecy was around 400 B.C. (see Chart F). From that time to the birth of Christ, God was silent as far as inspiring additional Scriptures to be written. Imagine yourself as one of the faithful Israelites—a small remnant—living around 400 B.C. Your Bible (the same as our present Old Testament) was divided into three main parts: law, prophets,

---

1. "Introduction to Matthew," in *The Westminster Study Edition of the Holy Bible* (Philadelphia: Westminster, 1948), p. 21.

and writings.[2] Read the last chapter appearing in each of those parts, and observe at least one promise of hope in each.
a) Law: Deuteronomy 34

---

b) Prophets: Malachi 4

---

c) Writings: 2 Chronicles 36

How is the Messiah identified in the first two passages? How is restored Jerusalem (2 Chron. 36) a type of the New Jerusalem, over which Christ shall one day reign? Do you think prophecies like these would have caused you to look forward to the "consolation of Israel," as Simeon did four hundred years later (Luke 2:25-35)?
2. Two prominent prophecies of the coming Messiah were that He would be a Jew and that He would be a descendant of King David. Hence the genealogy of Matthew 1:1-17, showing Jesus as son of Abraham (a Jew) and son of David (royal line). Read 1:1. Read the following Old Testament messianic prophecies:

Jesus as son of Abraham: Gen. 12:1, 3; 13:14-15; 22:15-18; Deut. 34:4

Jesus as son of David: 2 Sam. 7:8, 12-14 (cf. Heb. 1:5); 22:51; 23:1, 5; Pss. 89:3; 132:11-12; Isa. 55:3
3. Read the Old Testament prophecies that Matthew quotes or alludes to in the passage of this lesson. Complete the middle column.

O.T. PROPHECY	SUBJECT	N.T. FULFILLMENT
Isaiah 7:14		Matthew 1:22-23
Isaiah 11:1		Matthew 2:23 (see Notes)
Jeremiah 31:15		Matthew 2:17-18
Hosea 11:1		Matthew 2:15
Micah 5:2		Matthew 2:5-6

---

2. The content of the Jews' Old Testament is the same as that of our 39-book Old Testament. Because of various combinations of books (e.g., the twelve books by the minor prophets are counted as one book, called *The Twelve*), the Jewish Old Testament lists only twenty-four books. These are grouped under three headings: law, prophets, and writings.

4. Read Luke's genealogy of Christ (Luke 3:23-38) as preparation for studying Matthew's. Then study the comparative outline on Chart E.

GENEALOGIES OF CHRIST

Luke's list gives the bodily descent of Jesus,
   which could only be through Mary (Jesus being physically conceived
   of the Holy Spirit, not of Joseph).
This is Mary's genealogy.

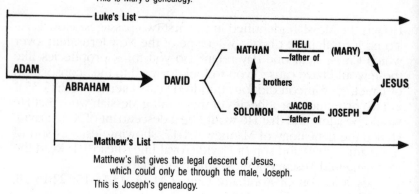

Matthew's list gives the legal descent of Jesus,
   which could only be through the male, Joseph.
This is Joseph's genealogy.

5. Read Matthew 1:17 and locate the three fourteen-generation periods on Chart F. This will be discussed later in the lesson.

II. ANALYSIS

Segments to be analyzed: 1:1-25; 2:1-23
Paragraph divisions: at verses 1:1, 18; 2:1, 13, 16, 19

A. General Analysis

Chart G is a work sheet on which you may record your observations of the Bible text, such as key words and phrases. Get in the habit early of noting such strong phrases (e.g., "God with us," 1:23) and recording them on paper.

Chart G shows the general contents of this passage. Try making other outlines similar to these.

What are your first impressions of these two chapters?

_____

_____

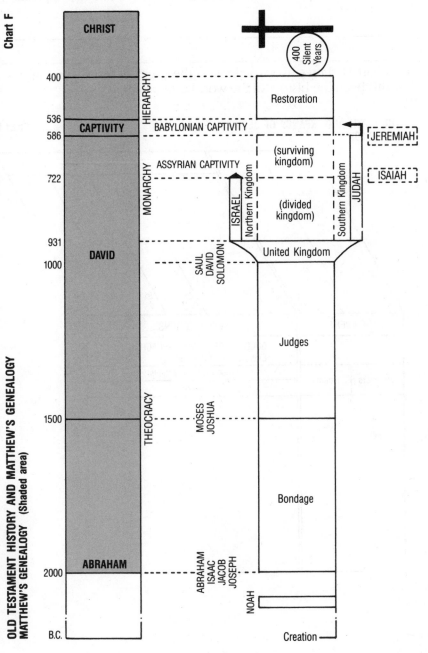

OLD TESTAMENT HISTORY AND MATTHEW'S GENEALOGY
MATTHEW'S GENEALOGY (Shaded area)

Chart F

Why do you think so much space is devoted to Herod's opposition to Jesus?

_____

_____

Chart G shows two reactions to the event of Jesus' coming. Has this been the history of the world ever since?

THE BIRTH AND INFANCY OF JESUS (1:1—2:23)   **Chart G**

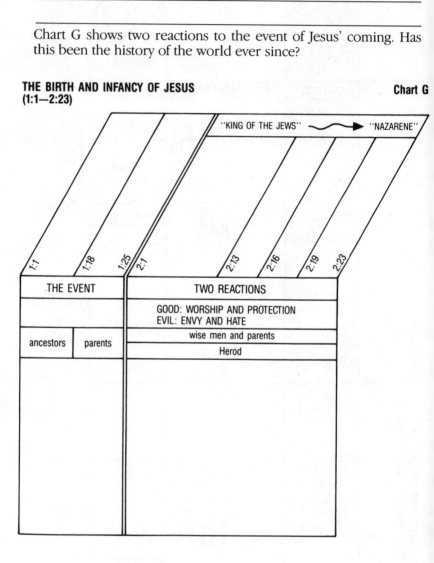

B. Paragraph Analysis

1. *Paragraph 1:1-17*
How far back in ancestry does this genealogy go?

_____

_____

Compare this with Luke's record (Luke 3:23-38). Account for Matthew's starting point.

_____

_____

What is the significant feature of the arrangement of Matthew's list (1:17)?

_____

_____

What do you think Matthew wants to emphasize: the numerical coincidence of the number fourteen or the three different experiences of Israel in Old Testament history? How would you describe those periods? (See Chart F for some help on this.)

_____

_____

What is so significant about Christ's arising out of such a history?

_____

2. *Paragraph 1:18-25*
Record what this paragraph reveals about the following:
(a) Jesus' parents

_____

(b) His conception

_____

(c) His birth

_____

(d) His names (1:21, 23)

_____

In what sense are the words of 1:21 a foundational statement of the gospel?

_____

_____

3. *Paragraph 2:1-12*

What do you learn here about the following?

(a) a true, seeking heart; a dishonest, proud heart

_____

(b) revelation by nature (miracle star); and revelation by Scripture (miracle Book)

_____

_____

(c) A classic example of "he that seeketh findeth" (Matt. 7:8)

_____

(d) the humble earthly origins of Jesus

_____

_____

(e) what true worship is

_____

How do you account for "all Jerusalem" being troubled over news of "his star" (2:2-3)?

_____

_____

4. *Paragraph 2:13-15*

What do you think went through the minds of Mary and Joseph when they heard that Herod would be seeking to murder their child?

_____

_____

5. *Paragraph 2:16-18*

What do these verses disclose about the wickedness of man?

_____

Why does God permit such cruel violence in the world?

_____

_____

6. *Paragraph 2:19-23*

A key phrase here is "He shall be called a Nazarene." (See *Notes*.) In Jesus' day, this was a term of scorn, prophesied in a general way in such passages as Isaiah 53:3 and Psalm 22:6. Compare John 1:46. Read Luke 2:1-7 to learn why Jesus' birth occurred in Bethlehem and not in Joseph's hometown, Nazareth.

III. NOTES

1. *"Joseph the husband of Mary, of whom was born Jesus"* (1:16). Thus Matthew carefully records Jesus birth as being of the virgin Mary, not of a begetting by Joseph. Jesus was conceived of the Holy Spirit (1:18, 20). Jesus' *legal* descent was through Joseph; His *physical* descent was through Mary.

2. *"Christ"* (1:16). This was the Greek word for Messiah, meaning literally "the anointed one." Read the prophecy of Isaiah 61:1-3, and observe the ministries that Jesus was anointed to perform.

3. *"Mary was espoused to Joseph"* (1:18). "Among the Jews, marriage vows were said at the betrothal, and required divorce to end them. Custom decreed an interval, usually a year, before the bride should take residence in her husband's house and physical union be consummated."[3]

4. *"Thou shalt call his name Jesus"* (1:21). The personal name "Jesus" is the Greek form of the Hebrew *Jeshua, Joshua,* or *Jehoshua,* meaning "Jehovah is salvation."

5. *"He shall save his people"* (1:21). To Joseph, the phrase "his people" could have meant only believing Israel. The larger intent of the phrase, however, is all who believe, whether Jew or Gentiles (John 3:16).

6. *"Wise men from the east"* (2:1). The Greek word translated "wise men" is *magoi.* The magi from lands east of Palestine were a caste specializing in astrology, medicine, and natural science. "It is entirely conceivable that these men had made contact with Jewish exiles, or with the prophecies and influence of Daniel, and thus were in possession of OT prophecies regarding Messiah."[4]

7. *"He shall be called a Nazarene"* (2:23). This exact statement is not to be found in any of the prophets. Some see Isaiah 11:1 and Jeremiah 23:5 as prophecies referred to here. In those verses the word "branch" is *netzer* in Hebrew, in which case "Nazarene" would be a word-play on the Hebrew. The other view is that Matthew is not quoting a particular prophecy but is rendering the general idea prophesied by various prophets (e.g., Isa. 53:3) that Jesus would be scorned and derided by men.

---

3. Homer A. Kent, "The Gospel According to Matthew," in *The Wycliffe Bible Commentary*, p. 932.
4. Ibid.

IV. FOR THOUGHT AND DISCUSSION

1. The human ancestors of Jesus were all sinners by nature, some being guilty of such gross acts as adultery and murder. How could Jesus' nature be preserved from defilement by such a relationship?

2. How does Jesus save people from their sins? What does it mean to be saved?

3. What does this passage teach about God's direction and providence for His children?

4. Make a list of other practical spiritual lessons taught by this passage.

V. FURTHER STUDY

Consult such outside helps as commentaries for an extended study of the two genealogies of Matthew and Luke and the prophecies and fulfillments of Hosea 11:1 (Egypt) and Jeremiah 31:15 (Ramah).

VI. WORDS TO PONDER

They shall call his name Emmanuel ... God with us (1:23).

Preparation of the King

Matthew skips the next thirty years of Jesus' life and reports Jesus' first public introduction to the multitudes. The announcer was John the Baptist, whose ministry of preparing Jesus' way was also prophesied by Old Testament prophets.

I. PREPARATION FOR STUDY

1. Read Isaiah 40:3-5. Chapters 40-66 of Isaiah are that book's "gospel" section, so it is appropriate that John the Baptist's coming is prophesied in the early verses of that section, even as he appears in the opening chapters of the New Testament gospels. (All four gospels report much about this forerunner of Christ.)

2. Consult a Bible dictionary for descriptions of the religious beliefs of the Pharisees and Sadducees.

II. ANALYSIS

Segment to be analyzed: 3:1–4:11
Paragraph divisions: at verses 3:1, 7, 13; 4:1

A. General Analysis

1. After you have marked the paragraph divisions in your Bible, read the passage through once or twice, underlining key words and phrases. What is the main theme of each paragraph? Record this on the work sheet of Chart H, which is a partially completed analytical chart. Study the outlines already shown on the work sheet. (Note: these work sheets appear from time to time throughout the manual. Use them as places to record your own observations. Anything you record—whether isolated words or related notes—will be of value to you in your studies.)

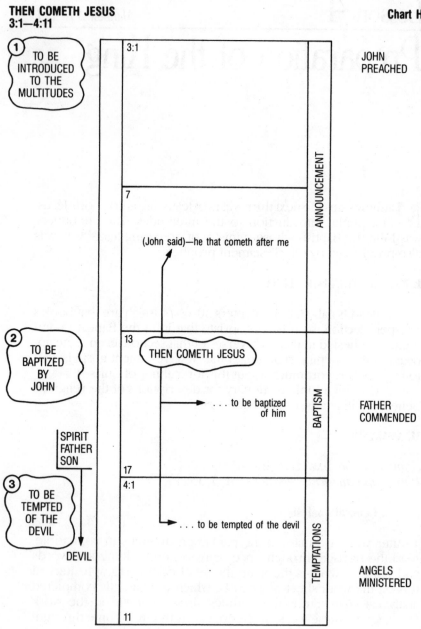

① TO BE INTRODUCED TO THE MULTITUDES

② TO BE BAPTIZED BY JOHN

SPIRIT
FATHER
SON

③ TO BE TEMPTED OF THE DEVIL

DEVIL

3:1

7

(John said)—he that cometh after me

13

THEN COMETH JESUS

. . . to be baptized of him

17

4:1

. . . to be tempted of the devil

11

ANNOUNCEMENT

BAPTISM

TEMPTATIONS

JOHN PREACHED

FATHER COMMENDED

ANGELS MINISTERED

28

2. Summarize what is said by each of the following in the segment.

(a) John the Baptist

_____

(b) Isaiah

_____

(c) People of Judea

_____

(d) Pharisees and Sadducees

_____

(e) Jesus

_____

(f) The Father

_____

(g) The devil

_____

B. Paragraph Analysis

1. *Paragraphs 3:1-6; 7-12*
What was the main message of John to the people? (3:2)

_____

How did such a ministry prepare the way for the coming of Jesus?
(In answering this, consider the effects of John's preaching, 3:5-6.)

_____

_____

Compare John's baptizing ministry (3:6, 11) with the ministry he
foretold Jesus would accomplish (3:11-12).

_____

_____

What was John's strong message to the religious leaders (3:7-12)?

_____

_____

What was their basic sin?

_____

_____

What did John preach about fruit in verses 8, 10, and 12?

_____

Follow this outline in the Bible text:
    (a) no righteousness (3:6)
    (b) self-righteousness (3:9)
    (c) true righteousness (3:15)
What ministry of Jesus does John prophesy in 3:11-12?

_____

Note the repetition of the pronouns "he" and "his."
2. *Paragraph 3:13-17*
Why was Jesus baptized by John (3:15)?

_____

_____

What did Jesus mean by His answer to John's question?

_____

What spiritual truths are suggested or explicitly taught by the following phrases of the text?
(a) "Jesus . . . went up straightway" (3:16)

_____

_____

(b) "the heavens were opened unto him" (3:16)

_____

_____

(c) "Spirit . . . descending like a dove" (3:16; cf. Isa. 11:2; Matt. 10:16)

_____

(d) "in whom I am well pleased" (3:17; cf. 17:5)

_____

_____

3. *Paragraph 4:1-11*
Summarize the content of this paragraph by completing Chart I. Were these *real* temptations for Jesus?

_____

Did He yield to any? _____

Were the temptations similar to any that came to Jesus later during the course of His earthly career? (Luke 4:13 reads that the devil "departed from him for a season.")

_____

What do you think were the purposes of His temptations?

_____

WILDERNESS TEMPTATIONS OF JESUS (4:1-11)				Chart I
MATTHEW'S ORDER	THE IF'S	THE ACTUAL TEMPTATION	REALM OF TEMPTATION	JESUS ANSWERS BY SCRIPTURE
① STONES				(Deut. 8:3)
② PINNACLE				(Ps. 91:11-12; Deut. 6:16)
③ KINGDOMS				(Deut. 6:13)

Why did Satan want Jesus to declare independence of His Father?

_____

III. NOTES

1. *"Kingdom of heaven"* (3:2). This expression is found only in Matthew. In parallel passages in the other gospels (e.g., Mark 1:15; Luke 8:10), it reads "kingdom of God." Walter Dunnett comments, "In a Gospel which is distinctively Jewish, it can best be understood as a euphemism, as the Jews hesitated to use the divine Name."[1] Compare Daniel 2:44 for Old Testament background to the phrase. (See the section *Further Study.*)

1. Walter M. Dunnett, *An Outline of New Testament Survey*, p. 29n.

2. *"Make his paths straight"* (3:3). Read Isaiah 40:3-4. In Bible times, when a high official was scheduled to ride through an area in his chariot, servants went ahead to clear the road of obstacles and to level it off if necessary. This is an appropriate picture of John's task to prepare people's hearts for the approaching ministry of Christ.

3. *"All Judea... were baptized of him [John]"* (3:5-6). The outward form of baptism in religious circles did not originate with John. But he attached a new significance to the rite, in its being the people's testimony of acceptance of John's kingdom message and a confession of sins in repentance. The later Christian baptisms extended this symbol to its highest significance.

4. *"Pharisees and Sadducees"* (3:7). These were the two religious groups most hostile to Jesus. Comparisons are shown below.

PHARISEES	SADDUCEES
name means "the separated ones"	name may be from a word meaning "the righteous ones"
largest and most influential sect	
extreme legalism	the aristocratic minority
little interest in politics	external legalism
believed in immortality, resurrection, spirits, and angels	a major concern with politics
	denied these doctrines
regarded rabbinic tradition highly	accepted as authoritative only the written Old Testament

5. *"To fulfil all righteousness"* (3:15). Jesus' water baptism symbolized in part His greater baptism at Calvary (20:22), in taking the sinner's place. By His death he fulfilled the requirements of God's righteous law. By His resurrection came the seal of the Father's acceptance of His substitutionary sacrifice.

6. *"Wilderness"* (4:1). The traditional site of this wilderness is the barren wasteland bordering the northwest end of the Dead Sea. The famous Dead Sea Scrolls were discovered in caves of this general region.

7. *"The devil"* (4:1). The name means "slanderer." The name "Satan" (v. 10) means "adversary."

8. *"It is written"* (4:4). The Greek tense is stronger: "it has been written," implying "it stands written." It is significant that the first recorded words of Jesus as He entered into the arena of public ministry are a strong assertion of the inviolable authority of Scripture.

IV. FOR THOUGHT AND DISCUSSION

1. The phrase "Repent ye" (3:2) means "Turn ye." What is repentance? Read Isaiah 55:7; Ezekiel 33:11, 14; Joel 2:12.

2. What do you think is meant by the phrase "He shall baptize you with the Holy Ghost [Spirit], and with fire" (3:11)?

3. What are the important spiritual lessons for the Christian as taught by Jesus' wilderness temptations (cf. Heb. 2:18; 4:14-16)? Ponder the truth that Jesus' temptations were of the kind Satan uses to assault Christians. "Jesus repulsed the mightiest blows of Satan not by a thunderbolt from heaven, but by the written Word of God employed in the wisdom of the Holy Spirit, A MEANS AVAILABLE TO EVERY CHRISTIAN."[2]

4. Cite an example of everyday living where a person "tempts" God by doing a rash deed and expecting God to protect (4:6-7).

V. FURTHER STUDY

Three subjects are suggested for extended study.

1. Make a comparative study of the New Testament phrases "kingdom of heaven" and "kingdom of God."[3]

2. Compare the man John the Baptist (also called John the Baptizer) with the prophet Elijah (e.g., 2 Kings 1:8).

3. Study the word "righteousness" in the Old Testament. It is interesting that this key word is in the first sentence of Jesus' utterances as recorded by Matthew.

VI. WORDS TO PONDER

Bread won't feed men's souls: obedience to every word of God is what we need (4:4, *The Living Bible*).

---

2. Homer A. Kent, "The Gospel According to Matthew," in *The Wycliffe Bible Commentary*, p. 935.
3. The English word "kingdom" is a contraction of the phrase "king's domain." Consult W. E. Vine, *An Expository Dictionary of New Testament Words*, 2:294-96, for a discussion of the two phrases noted above.

Lesson 5

Sermon on the Mount

Matthew has now reached the place in his account where he can begin to report Jesus' discourses. We saw in lessons 1 and 2 that five great discourses are a prominent feature of this gospel. The Sermon on the Mount, studied in this lesson, is the first of these. We also observed in earlier studies that Matthew does not follow a strict chronological order in his reporting, especially in the first half of the book, because his interest is primarily topical, in line with devoting so much space to the discourses. This structure will be apparent in our study of this lesson.

I. PREPARATION FOR STUDY

1. Review Chart B, and recall that Matthew does not report most of the first year of Jesus' public ministry. Only John (John 1-4) reports the early Judean ministry. The passage of this lesson opens Jesus' early Galilean ministry. (Read Matt. 4:12.)

2. Read Isaiah 9:1-2, which Matthew freely quotes in 4:14-16. Zabulon (Zebulun) and Nephthalim (Naphtali) were two tribes of Israel in Old Testament times that settled in the areas later to be known as Lower Galilee and Upper Galilee, respectively. Look again at the map and fix in your mind the following locations cited in the present passage: Nazareth (4:13); Capernaum (4:13); Syria (4:24); Decapolis (4:25); Perea—"beyond Jordan" (4:25).

3. Consult a Bible dictionary for a description of the Jewish scribes. Jesus often associated the scribes with the Pharisees (e.g., 5:20).

4. Read Luke 3:19-24 for background to Matthew 4:12 (John's imprisonment).

5. Review the survey Chart D and recall that 4:12 begins a new major division in Matthew's account. What title is given to this division on the chart?

II. ANALYSIS

Passages to be analyzed: 4:12-25; 5:1–7:29
Segment divisions: at verses 4:12; 5:1, 17; 6:1, 19; 7:1, 13[1]

A. General Analysis (4:12-25)

1. Read 4:12-25, noting the many geographical references. How many times does the name Galilee appear?

_____

2. Matthew includes this passage to give some historical setting to the Sermon on the Mount, which he reports in detail. This context is shown in the diagram below.

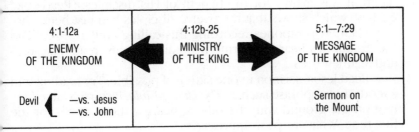

4:1-12a	4:12b-25	5:1—7:29
ENEMY OF THE KINGDOM	MINISTRY OF THE KING	MESSAGE OF THE KINGDOM
Devil { —vs. Jesus —vs. John		Sermon on the Mount

What parts of this segment are of a general nature, summarizing the ministries of Jesus in Galilee at this time?

_____

_____

B. Paragraph Analysis

1. *Paragraph 4:12-17*
What is the significance of the word "Gentiles" (4:15) in this early reference to Jesus' ministry?

_____

What bright word of Isaiah's prophecy describes Jesus' ministry?

_____

What message did Jesus preach?

_____

1. The segment divisions shown here appear on Chart J.

35

2. *Paragraphs 4:18-22*
What are the prominent truths of this account?

_____

_____

_____

3. *Paragraph 4:23-25*
What threefold ministry did Jesus perform?

_____

_____

4. *Paragraph 5:1–7:29*
Jesus preached this sermon on a mountain probably near Capernaum. It was mainly for the benefit of His disciples. (Read Luke
6:12-20, which shows that the twelve disciples had just been chosen. Matthew postpones recording this calling until 10:1-42.) Did
the multitudes hear the sermon? To answer this, read Luke 6:17
and Matthew 7:28.

Read Jesus' sermon in one sitting, if possible. Try reading it in
a modern paraphrase such as *The Living Bible*. Picture yourself sitting on the ground with the others, hearing these words for the
first time. What are your impressions?

_____

_____

_____

Did Jesus preach the sermon to tell how a person can become a
Christian or how a person already a believer should live the Christian life?

_____

_____

This sermon may be outlined in various ways.[2] Chart J suggest an
arrangement of thought.
Note the title given to the sermon. Early in His ministry, Jesus
wanted to make clear to His disciples and to the multitudes just
what kind of kingdom He had come to establish.

---

2. Parts of the sermon are also reported by Luke. It is possible that Jesus said other things at this time, not reported by the gospels. The writers did not intend
   to be exhaustive (cf. John 20:30-31).

What the Kingdom Is All About

5:3		5:17	5:48	6:1		7:13	7:27
KINGDOM CITIZENS		KINGDOM LAWS		KINGDOM ATTITUDES AND DEEDS		CONCLUDING EXHORTATIONS	
	5:13		5:21		6:19		
Their Character	Their Influence	The Law's Ful- fillment	The Old and the New	WORSHIP —giving —praying —fasting	WALK	Citizenship Tested	

Scan the three chapters of Matthew, and observe how the outlines of Chart J grow out of the text. This exercise will give you a good general grasp of the passage.

Selected questions on the various segments and paragraphs are given below. Let these be starters for study. Expand your studies beyond these exercises. Refer often to the outline of Chart J for reminder of context.

(a) *Kingdom citizens* (5:3-16)

These sayings of Jesus are called beatitudes. Read how the *Amplified Bible* expands on the meaning of the word "blessed." What do you think of when you read this word in the Bible?

_____

_____

Having described the *character* of Christians (5:3-12), Jesus now shows what *influence* they should have in the world (5:13-16). What two metaphors does He use to get across His point?

_____

_____

Complete the following work sheet.

THE BEATITUDES OF 5:3-12				
	Verse	Description	Promise	Present-Day Application
IN HEART	3			
	4			
	5			
	6			
IN OUTREACH	7			
	8			
	9			
	10			
	11-12			

Make a list of practical applications taught here.

_____

_____

_____

(b) *Kingdom laws* (5:17-48)
The Jews hearing Jesus preach this sermon wondered how He looked upon the Old Testament Scriptures and its many laws. It was a legitimate question, and Jesus spent no little time answering it.

The first paragraph (5:17-20) identifies God's law in general; its unchanging, timeless demands upon man; and Christ's relationship to it. Study these three subjects in the paragraph.

The remaining paragraphs (5:21-48) show Christ applying the principles of 5:17-20 to various life situations. Record your studies below.

Paragraph	O.T. Law	Jesus' Application	Further Applications
5:21-26			
5:27-32			
5:33-37			
5:38-42			
5:43-47			
5:48	"Be ye therefore perfect, even as your Father in heaven is perfect"		

What help does the Christian have to fulfill Jesus' commands of these paragraphs?

_____

_____

How is 5:48 a concluding verse to 5:17-48?

_____

_____

What does Jesus mean by the word "perfect"? Is He commanding the impossible?

(c) *Kingdom attitudes and deeds* (6:1–7:12)
This section is of two parts, as shown on Chart J: workshop (6:1-18) and walk (6:19–7:12). What three aspects of worship does Jesus discuss in 6:1-18?

_____

_____

Look in the text for references to motive, manner, and reward of each activity. Consider the following.

    GIVING: the outward look
        Give as unto God: not trumpet giving; not tabulation giving
    PRAYING: the upward look
        Pray as unto God: not hypocrite praying; not heathen praying
    FASTING: the inward look
        Fast as unto God: not mask mourning; not public parade

Spend much time studying the paragraph on prayer (6:5-15).
What is the general subject of 6:19-34?

List various practical truths taught here. Do the same for the next two paragraphs (7:1-6 and 7:7-12).

(d) *Concluding exhortations* (7:13-27)
What is the subject of each paragraph?
7:13-14

7:15-23

7:24-27

What is common to all three?

Note the contrasts: wide and narrow; false and true; wise and foolish.
Do you see any others? Why do many contrasts appear in the Bible?

How is this section a fitting conclusion to Jesus' sermon?

What was the general effect of Jesus' sermon on the multitudes?
(7:28-29; 8:1).

_____

_____

III. NOTES

1. *"Meek"* (5:5). Jesus said of Himself, "I am meek and lowly
in heart" (11:29). Jesus' meekness was not weakness or backward-
ness but gentleness of strength, power under control.

2. *"Not to destroy, but to fulfill"* (5:17). Jesus fulfilled the Old
Testament by keeping God's law perfectly; by fulfilling its type and
prophecies; and by paying the full penalty of death in the place of
sinners, which the law demands.

3. *"Jot . . . tittle"* (5:18). Jot was the smallest Hebrew letter
(yodh). Tittle was a small extension on a Hebrew letter, barely visi-
ble to the eye.

4. *"Raca"* (5:22). This is probably an Aramaic word meaning
"empty." Two modern translations of the word: "simpleton";
"idiot."

5. *"Compel thee to go a mile"* (5:41). This is a reference to a
custom that allowed public postal couriers to compel a person to
do an errand (cf. Matt. 27:32).

6. *"Be ye therefore perfect"* (5:48). The word translated "perfect" is from *telos*, meaning "end, goal, limit." One modern translation reads, "You must become spiritually mature."

7. *"Forgive us our debts"* (6:12). The word "debts" is a correct
translation, even as "trespasses" is correctly translated in verse 14.
The phrase refers to our spiritual indebtedness to God because of
transgression against Him.

8. *"When ye fast"* (6:16). The Mosaic law of Jesus' hearers pre-
scribed one annual day of fasting, the Day of Atonement (Lev.
16:29-31; cf. Isa 58:3 on the phrase "afflict your soul"). The Pharisees observed two fasts weekly as a public exhibition of their pro-
fessed piety. Jesus no doubt had Pharisees in mind when He said,
"Be not as the hypocrites" (6:16).

9. *"Mammon"* (6:24). This is a transliteration of an Aramaic
word for riches. It is derived from a root meaning "that in which
one trusts." Compare the word "Amen," which comes from the
same root but is used in a different sense.

10. *"Sufficient unto the day is the evil thereof"* (6:34). The
New American Standard Bible reads, "Each day has enough trou-
ble of its own."

41

IV. FOR THOUGHT AND DISCUSSION

The passage of this lesson is a gold mine of spiritual truths that can be applied to everyday living. In your own words, what does it teach about the following subjects? (The list is selective; add others.)

The happy Christian
The Christian with an effective witness
The place of the Old Testament in the Christian life
The commands of the Old and New testaments compared
Whether or not fasting is for Christians
Righteous motives in giving and fasting
How a Christian should pray
The Christian's attitude regarding material goods
Criticizing others
The way into God's kingdom

V. FURTHER STUDY

Many devotional books have been written on the Sermon on the Mount and on the Lord's Prayer. You may want to devote further time reading such books.

VI. WORD TO PONDER

Your Father knoweth what things ye have need of, before ye ask him (6:8).

Lesson 6
Power of the King

Matthew has reported an important early discourse of Jesus: now he will show how Jesus' works supported His words. The people who heard or overheard the Sermon on the Mount could rightly ask, "Can this man accomplish what He talks about?" One of the main purposes of Jesus' miracles was to attest His divine power, demonstrating that He was the Son of God, the Messiah sent from above. His greatest mission was to save people from their sins. But if He could not perform physical miracles, then He surely could not perform spiritual miracles, the more difficult task (cf. 9:5).

For this section of his account about the *power* of the King, Matthew selected various miracles from Jesus' public career, reporting them in a nonchronological order.[1] Matthew's main interest was the *subject* of miracle-working, not the particular *order* of their occurrences. Observe on Chart K that Matthew 8:1–9:34 reports three groups of three paragraphs on miracles, each group separated from the others by paragraphs about discipleship.

I. PREPARATION FOR STUDY

Review the survey Chart D, noting where the narrative section of this lesson falls in Matthew's gospel. What are the two discourse sections on either side of the narrative section?

---

1. A glance at a harmony of the gospels shows this random selectivity. (See the order in A.T. Robertson, *A Harmony of the Gospels for Student of the Life of Christ* [New York: Harper, 1922], p. xxxiv).

JESUS' MIRACLES
8:1—9:34

PASSAGE	OBJECTS OF MIRACLES	FAITH INVOLVED	JESUS' METHOD OF HEALING	SPIRITUAL INSTRUCTION	EFFECT
8:1-4	LEPER	"If thou wilt thou canst"	hand touch	—Jesus' desire —public testimony	(Matthew does not report. See Mark 1:45.)
5-13					
14:17					
DISCIPLESHIP: 8:18-22					
23:27					
28:34					
9:1-8					
DISCIPLESHIP: 9:9-13 and 9:14-17					
18-26					
27-31					
32-34					

II. ANALYSIS

Segment to be analyzed: 8:1–9:34
Paragraph divisions: at verses 8:1, 5, 14, 18, 23, 28; 9:1, 9, 14, 18, 27, 32

A. General Analysis: Jesus' Miracles

As noted earlier, the work sheet of Chart K shows how 8:1–9:34 is organized into three groups of three paragraphs about miracles. The intervening paragraphs on discipleship are also shown. Read the entire passage, and record the items called for on the work sheet. An example is shown. This exercise will give you a good view of the segment. Arrive at some general and specific conclusions about Jesus' miracle-working. For example, did He always use the same external method?

B. Paragraph Analysis: Discipleship

1. *Paragraph 8:18-22*
This paragraph records two brief conversations of Jesus with two different men. What is taught here about discipleship?

_____

2. *Paragraphs 9:9-13, 14-17*
The first paragraph is about eating; the second, about fasting. What is common to both paragraphs? For example note the two questions of "why."

_____

_____

What do these paragraphs teach about discipleship?

_____

_____

_____

What do you think of when you read or hear the words "Follow me" (9:9)?

_____

_____

45

III. NOTES

1. *"Children of the kingdom"* (8:12). This is a general reference to Jews to whom the kingdom prophecies were originally given. Jesus' point in this context is that even Jews with such a heritage will be separated from God for their unbelief, in contrast to the salvation of Gentiles, like the centurion, who believe.

2. *"Possessed with devils"* (8:16). The translation "devils" should read "demons." There is one devil but hosts of demons (cf. Rev. 20:10).

3. "Himself took our infirmities" (8:17). The messianic prophecy of Isaiah 53:4 refers to two healings: physical and spiritual. Jesus can heal disease (one of the effects of sin) as well as deal with its ultimate cause (sin itself).[2] Compare 1 Peter 2:24.

4. *"Suffer me first to . . . bury my father"* (8:21). The intention here could be to stay at home until the father's death. Jesus' reply (8:22) would cover even the more grievous circumstance that the father had just died. G. Campbell Morgan writes, "Loyalty of discipleship to Christ is loyalty to the uttermost. Thus sacrifice is inevitable, such as putting the tender ties of family relationship in submission to Christ. Christ's claim was always the claim of an absolute supremacy. He never admitted that any other tie of affection could be allowed for a moment to interfere with the soul's loyalty to Himself."[3] When loyalty to Christ is put first, then He enables His servant also to fulfill obligations of love and care. Recall how Abraham was willing to sacrifice his beloved son Isaac (Gen. 22).

5. *"This man blasphemeth"* (9:3). Mark 2:7 shows why the people charged Jesus with blasphemy.

6. *"Many publicans and sinners . . . sat down with him"* (9:10). "It was a strange medley at Levi's feast (Jesus and the four fisher disciples; Nathaniel and Philip; Matthew Levi and his former companions, publicans and sinners; Pharisees with their scribes or students as onlookers; disciples of John the Baptist who were fasting at the very time that Jesus was feasting)."[4]

7. *"Children of the bridechamber"* (9:15). This may be a reference to the wedding guests, or to friends or attendants of the bridegroom.

8. *"New . . . old"* (9:16-17). The principle expressed in these verses is that "Jesus Christ has come to bring in a new dispensa-

2. Homer A. Kent, "The Gospel According to Matthew," in *The Wycliffe Bible Commentary,* pp. 942-43.
3. G. Campbell Morgan, *The Gospel According to Matthew,* p. 88.
4. A. T. Robertson, *Word Pictures in the New Testament,* 1:72.

tion altogether, which cannot be fitted into the forms of the old Jewish economy."[5]

9. *"The maid is not dead, but sleepeth"* (9:24). The maid was really dead physically, but because Jesus knew He was shortly going to revive her to life, He referred to her state as *sleep*. In the same way, Paul refers to the bodies of the dead in Christ as being asleep in Jesus (1 Thess. 4:14-16).

IV. FOR THOUGHT AND DISCUSSION

1. If you are studying in a group, discuss the important lessons and examples of discipleship which appear in this passage.

2. How did Jesus look upon physical disease of people, and how did He view their spiritual disease of sin?

3. Does God perform instantaneous physical healings today, similar to those recorded in this passage? If so, what are the conditions?

V. FURTHER STUDY

Two subjects suggested for extended study are:
1. demonism: in New Testament times, and today
2. the intermediate state of believers and unbelievers, between death and the end of time

VI. WORDS TO PONDER

Cheer up, son! For I have forgiven your sins! (9:2*b; The Living Bible*).

---

5. B. F. C. Atkinson, "The Gospel According to Matthew," in *The New Bible Commentary*, p. 785.

Commission to the Twelve

Jesus knew that His ministry to the multitudes would not continue for much longer. He must choose disciples to be His witnesses after He returned to His Father. The disciples in turn must train others whom He would call by His Spirit and send forth into the world's harvest field.

Of the four gospels, Matthew records the most of Jesus' instructions to His twelve disciples. Many lessons about discipleship can be learned from the passage of this lesson.

I. PREPARATION FOR STUDY

1. Refer back to Chart B and observe the notation "Jesus ordains twelve" at the beginning of the middle Galilean period. This is when the twelve were first called, as reported in Mark 3:13-19 and Luke 6:12-16. Matthew does not record the list of twelve names until the time of this present passage, which was toward the end of the middle Galilean period. In your Bible, mark 10:2-4 as a parenthesis. Then read 10:5 after 10:1, and you will catch the continuity of Matthew's reporting.

2. Read Matthew 24:8-31 as an introduction to 10:16-23 (one of the paragraphs of this lesson).

3. Consult a Bible dictionary for a description of the Samaritans. Note especially why Samaritans were not classified as Jews in Jesus' day.

II. ANALYSIS

Segment to be analyzed: 9:35–11:1
Paragraph divisions: at verses 9:35; 10:1, 16, 24, 34, 40

9:35	SETTING
10:1	COMMISSION
day of judgment	
16	
Son of man be come	
24	COUNSEL
before my Father	
34	
shall lose . . . shall find	
40	
11:1 reward	

A. General Analysis

1. Use the work sheet of Chart L for recording your studies of this paragraph. Note how the segment is divided into three parts. Follow procedures of study suggested in earlier lessons.

2. Beginning with the second paragraph, observe how each paragraph ends with a reference to the far future (e.g., "day of judgment," 10:15).

B. Paragraph Analysis

1. *Paragraph 9:35-38*
What does this paragraph teach about the following?
(1) Jesus' ministry

_____

(b) Jesus' compassion

_____

(c) the harvest field

_____

2. *Paragraph 10:1-15*
How were Jesus' and the disciples' missions similar?

_____

_____

Account for the instructions of these verses.
10:5-6

_____

10:9-10

_____

10:14

_____

3. *Paragraph 10:16-23*
List the things Jesus taught His disciples about persecution.

_____

_____

_____

_____

What does Jesus say in verse 23 that suggests He was projecting the application of these words especially on the screen of the end times?

_____

_____

Compare this paragraph and 24:8-31, read earlier. Atkinson writes about verse 23:

> These rather difficult words seem to lift the commission here given to the apostles out of purely local circumstances and prove its application to the missionary work of the whole Church in every generation.[1]

4. *Paragraph 10:24-33*
Observe the repeated phrase "Fear not." What antidote for fear does Jesus prescribe?

_____

_____

What counsel does Jesus give in these verses?
10:24-25

_____

10:27

_____

10:32-33

_____

5. *Paragraph 10:34-39*
Account for the strong teaching of 10:34-36.

_____

_____

What do verses 37-39 teach about discipleship?

_____

_____

_____

1. B.F.C. Atkinson, "The Gospel According to Matthew," in *The New Bible Commentary*, p. 786.

6. Paragraph 10:40–11:1
Which is your favorite verse in this paragraph?

_____

_____

What is taught here about reward?

_____

III. NOTES

1. *"Go not into the way of the Gentiles"* (10:5). In the divine timetable the Jews were to hear the gospel first, then the Gentiles (Cf. Rom. 1:16; 2:9-11; Gen. 12:2-3). Read Matthew 28:19 and Acts 1:8 for the words of Jesus that extended the commission to proclaim the gospel to everyone.

2. *"Shake off the dust of your feet"* (10:14). This was a symbolic gesture, with a purpose of warning. In effect, the disciples were saying to those refusing a hearing, as Paul said at a later time, "Your blood be upon your own heads" (Acts 18:6).

3. *"Fear him which is able to destroy both soul and body in hell"* (10:28). This is a reference to God, not Satan.

4. *"I came not to send peace, but a sword"* (10:34). Christ's coming did not alleviate or wipe out sin. Instead, the awfulness of sin was revealed. His death on the cross is bold evidence of this. However, Christ *did* come to offer peace to all who confess their sins and accept Him into their hearts. Read John 14:27; 16:33; 20:19, 21, 26; Acts 10:36.

5. *"He that taketh not his cross"* (10:38). This is the first of twenty-eight appearances of the word "cross" in the New Testament. When Jesus spoke these words at this time, He knew that crucifixion would be His manner of dying, but His disciples did not know it. However, later they would see the deep significance of such a statement (cf. Gal. 2:20).

IV. FOR THOUGHT AND DISCUSSION

What practical lessons do you learn from the following selected verses?

9:36

_____

9:37-38

_____

10:16

_____

10:19-20

_____

10:22

_____

10:24

_____

10:29-31

_____

10:42

_____

V. FURTHER STUDY

With the help of a Bible dictionary, learn all you can about each of the twelve disciples. Concerning Judas Iscariot, do you think he ever was a genuine believer?

VI. WORDS TO PONDER

If you cling to your life, you will lose it; but if you give it up for Me, you will save it (10:39, *The Living Bible*).

Rejection of the King

J esus' popularity reached a peak around the middle of the second year of His public ministry. Large multitudes pressed Him from every side because of His miracles and the authority of His preaching and teaching. When opposition began to set in, it was mainly from Jewish religious leaders who rejected His claim as being the Messiah from heaven, the King of the promised kingdom. By the time the middle Galilean period was over (see Chart B), Jesus foresaw a dark road ahead: envy and hate at its worst, eventually leading to Calvary. In the passage of this lesson, Matthew has reported various incidents when Jesus' opponents began to challenge His claims. Jesus' replies to His enemies reveal much about the basic spiritual problems of man at that time, which are the same as the ones we face today.

I. PREPARATION FOR STUDY

1. Recall that Matthew does not follow a strict chronological order in the first half of his account. Our present passage illustrates this. At 11:2 Matthew reaches back into early months of the middle Galilean period, before the events of 9:35–11:1. Then at 14:1, he picks up the chronological sequence again. (Try reading 11:1 followed immediately by 14:1.)

2. Review Chart D again, noting how 11:2–12:50 fits into the overall structure of Matthew's account.

II. ANALYSIS

Segment to be analyzed: 11:2–12:50
Paragraph divisions: at verses 11:2, 7, 20, 25; 12:1, 9, 15, 22, 38, 46

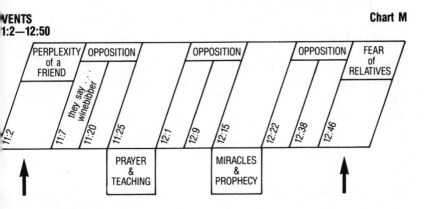

A. General Analysis

A survey of this passage shows a symmetry of content in the events that Matthew chose to report. Observe this symmetrical arrangement in Chart M. (The ten oblique spaces represent the ten paragraphs of the segment.)

1. According to the chart, which paragraphs record opposition to Jesus? Read these paragraphs in your Bible, underlining each instance of opposition. Record a short phrase on the chart showing the subject of opposition (an example is given).

2. Note how the first and last paragraphs are identified on the chart. These paragraphs will be discussed later. For now, read the Bible text.

3. What two paragraphs in the central part of the segment do not record opposition? Read the paragraphs in your Bible. What does each of these paragraphs add to the overall subject of the passage?

_____

_____

_____

4. Make a comparative study of the oppositions of this segment. Identify the following in each case:

occasion and setting	accusers
object of accusation	Jesus' reply
whom addressed	result
accusation	

B. Paragraph Analysis

1. *Paragraph 11:2-6*
Do you think John had lost faith in Jesus?[1] To answer this, read what Jesus says about John in the next paragraph.
What is John's basic question (11:3)? Jesus' reply in verses 4-6 supplies an answer to this. (Read Isa. 35:5; 61:1 in connection with Jesus' reply.)

_____

_____

2. *Paragraph 11:7-19*
What do you learn about John from these verses?

_____

_____

What do verses 17-19 reveal about many people who hear the gospel?

_____

_____

3. *Paragraph 11:20-24*
In what way was Jesus rejected by the people described in this paragraph?

_____

Compare 11:20 with 11:17.

_____

4. *Paragraph 11:25-30*
View this paragraph as related immediately to the previous one. This connection is suggested by the following outline:
    (a) pronouncement of judgment (11:20-24)
    (b) praise to God (11:25-26)
    (c) testimony of Jesus (11:26-27)
    (d) invitation of Jesus (11:28-30)

1. See the reading of 11:3 in *Today's English Version* for the suggestion that John asked the question especially for the benefit of his disciples.

How does this paragraph describe those who do *not* reject Jesus, as contrasted with the unbelievers of 11:20-24?

_____

_____

5. *Paragraph 12:1-8*
Read the following passages for background to this paragraph.
    Old Testament rules: Lev. 24:9; Ex. 20:10; Deut. 23:25
    David: 1 Sam. 21:1-6
    priests: Num. 28:9-10
    mercy: Hos. 6:6 (cf. Matt. 9:13)
How does 12:8 summarize Jesus' reply to the Pharisees?

_____

6. *Paragraph 12:9-14*
What basic principle does Jesus teach in 12:12?

_____

_____

Note the intensity of opposition in 12:14. How do you account for this?

_____

_____

7. *Paragraph 12:15-21*
Read the prophecy of Isaiah 42:1-4. What messianic picture of Jesus shows here?

_____

_____

Contrast this with the violent intentions described in 12:14.

_____

8. *Paragraph 12:22-37*
What does Jesus teach here about His own power?

_____

_____

about sins of the heart?

_____

about judgment?

_____

9. Paragraph 12:38-45
Read 1 Corinthians 1:22. What was the obstacle to faith in the heart of Jews?

_____

_____

In the heart of Gentiles?

_____

_____

What kind of sign were the scribes and Pharisees seeking (12:38)?

_____

How did Jesus expose their unbelief in these three examples?
    a) men of Nineveh (12:41; read John 3:5)
    b) queen of the south (12:42; read 1 Kings 10:1-13)
    c) demon-possessed man (12:43-45)[2]
How was the prophecy of 12:40 fulfilled in Jesus' life?

_____

_____

10. Paragraph 12:46-50
Read the parallel account of Mark 3:31-35, and include Mark 3:20-21. The word "friends" of 3:21 is correctly translated "relatives" in the *Berkeley Version*. These were probably "his brethren and his mother" of 3:31. What was their concern, or fear?

_____

_____

Keep this in mind when you study Matthew 12:46-50. What did Jesus intend to convey by His reply of 12:48-50?

_____

_____

III. NOTES

1. *"Do we look for another"* (11:3). In asking this question, John was not disloyal but perplexed. For example, he may have been wondering why Jesus had not yet begun His judgment ministry of fire baptism (3:11-12).

2. *"A reed shaken with the wind"* (11:7). A wavering person would answer to such a description. John was not that kind.

---

2. Refer to a commentary for help in applying this parable to Israel's rejection of Christ.

3. *"Wisdom is justified of her children"* (11:19). The outward methods of John and Jesus were different, but the works of both of them were fruitful. For wisdom "is vindicated by her effects" (*Berkeley*).

4. *"It shall not be forgiven him"* (12:31-32). Some interpret the "unpardonable" sin as attributing to the devil the miraculous works of the Holy Spirit. Others see it as the ultimate refusal to believe on the testimony of the Spirit concerning Jesus Christ.[3] "He who rejects every overture of the Spirit removes himself from the only force that can lead him to forgiveness (John 3:36)."[4]

5. *"Three days and three nights"* (12:40). Jesus did not mean three twenty-four-hour periods. He was referring here to the three different days (part or whole), during which His body would be in the grave: Friday, Saturday, and Sunday.

6. *"The same is my brother, and sister, and mother"* (12:50). Jesus did not belittle His family relationships but exalted His spiritual ties with all believers above any blood relationship. His relationship as Son of man was infinitely more significant than His relationship as Son of Mary.

IV. FOR THOUGHT AND DISCUSSION

Go through these two chapters one final time and pick out favorite verses and phrases that suggest important spiritual lessons. Record these on paper, and meditate on them.

V. FURTHER STUDY

Study what the New Testament teaches about the function of Old Testament law. Romans and Galatians are two important sources on this.

VI. WORD TO PONDER

Wear my yoke—for it fits perfectly—and let me be your teacher . . . and you will find refreshment and blessed quiet for your souls. For the yoke I offer you is a kindly one, and the load I ask you to bear is light (11:29-30; selected paraphrases).

---

3. G. Campbell Morgan, *The Gospel According to Matthew*, p. 131.
4. Homer A. Kent, "The Gospel According to Matthew," in *The Wycliffe Bible Commentary*, p. 950.

Parables of the Kingdom

When Jesus had finished answering His opponents, He went down to the seaside to teach the multitudes. His favorite method of teaching was by parables (around forty are recorded in the gospels, in addition to many parabolic illustrations).[1] The Master Teacher well knew that the strongest witness of the gospel is the positive proclamation of its truth. Although He took time out to defend the gospel from the verbal attacks of His opponents, He spent most of His time teaching the doctrines of the kingdom.

I. PREPARATION FOR STUDY

1. This group of parables spoken on one particular occasion is the third main discourse of Matthew's account. (Do you recall what the two earlier ones were? See survey Chart D.) Jesus spoke these parables on what has since been called "The Busy Day." Mark 3:19–5:20 records all the events and discourses of that day. Read Mark 3:20, and note the reference to a house. This is where the actions of Matthew 12:22ff. took place. Now, at 13:1, Matthew writes that "the same day Jesus went out of the house, and sat by the sea side." He surely could have spent the rest of the day ministering at the house. What may have been His reasons for leaving there and going down to the shore?

2. A biblical parable has been described as "an earthly story with a heavenly meaning." It is a comparison of two things to convey a spiritual truth. It is revelation by illustration, to aid understanding, not to hinder it. Jesus did not teach the mysteries of the kingdom to the crowds, because they were not ready for deep

---

1. Lists and brief descriptions of all the parables appear in W. Graham Scroggie, *A Guide to the Gospels,* pages 278 -86; 549-51; 663-64.

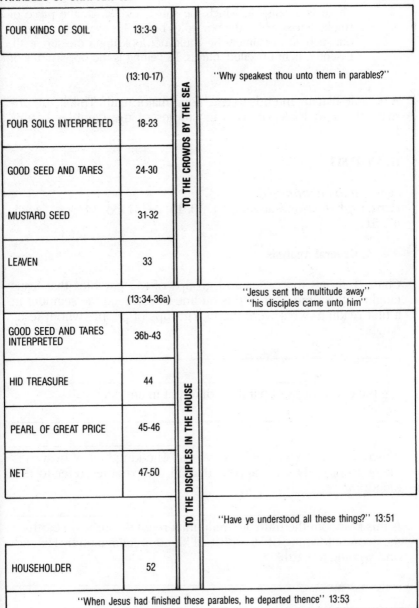

FOUR KINDS OF SOIL	13:3-9		
	(13:10-17)	TO THE CROWDS BY THE SEA	"Why speakest thou unto them in parables?"
FOUR SOILS INTERPRETED	18-23		
GOOD SEED AND TARES	24-30		
MUSTARD SEED	31-32		
LEAVEN	33		
	(13:34-36a)		"Jesus sent the multitude away" "his disciples came unto him"
GOOD SEED AND TARES INTERPRETED	36b-43	TO THE DISCIPLES IN THE HOUSE	
HID TREASURE	44		
PEARL OF GREAT PRICE	45-46		
NET	47-50		
			"Have ye understood all these things?" 13:51
HOUSEHOLDER	52		
"When Jesus had finished these parables, he departed thence" 13:53			

truths (13:10-15). Morgan illustrates this veiling aspect of parables by this contemporary parable.

> There is a sense in which the sun is hidden by the piece of smoked glass which the boy holds before his eyes, and yet without such an instrument he could not look upon the sun at all. Essential light unveiled, blinds. Its veiling is the opportunity of vision.[2]

A parable usually intends to teach one major truth. This is the primary thing to look for in your studies of the parables of this lesson.

II. ANALYSIS

Segment to be analyzed: 13:1-53
Paragraph divisions: at verses 1, 10, 18, 24, 31, 33, 34, 36*b*, 44, 45, 47, 51

A. General Analysis

Chart N shows the order and groups of the parables that Jesus taught at this time. Follow this outline as you read the segment in a first reading. What were the two groups of people whom Jesus taught?

_____

_____

Are the two groups of parables different in any way?

_____

_____

Which parables open with the words "The kingdom of heaven is likened unto"? Does it appear that all the parables refer to this kingdom?

_____

Is this kingdom the ultimate millennial reign of Christ on earth or the present forming of His spiritual kingdom climaxed by His second coming to earth?

_____

_____

2. G. Campbell Morgan, *The Gospel According to Matthew*, p. 141.

Use Chart N as a work sheet to record observations.

B. Paragraph Analysis

Only a few study exercises are suggested below. Extend your study beyond these.
1. *Paragraphs 13:1-9 and 13:18-23*[3]
How do the various types of sown seed illustrate the proclamation of the gospel today?

---

2. *Paragraph 13:10-17*
What do these verses reveal about Jesus' purpose in using parables to teach the crowds?

---

3. *Other Parables*
Record on Chart N the main point of the remainder of the parables. How is the last parable (householder) an appropriate conclusion to Jesus' instructions to the disciples?

III. NOTES

1. *"Hear ye . . . the parable of the sower"* (13:18). Jesus gave an explanation of this parable to His disciples (cf. 13:10), just as He expounded the meaning of the tares parable to them (13:36-43). Read Mark 4:34.
2. *"Tares"* (13:25). This is darnel, a noxious plant, resembling wheat in appearance until its ear appears.
3. *"Leaven"* (13:33). Leaven of this parable is usually interpreted and applied in one of two ways: either the permeating quality of the gospel or the ever-presence of evil, such as apostasy, in the church. The latter interpretation is based on various biblical references to leaven as evil (e.g., Matt. 16:6-12; Mark. 8:15; 1 Cor.

---

3. This is an example of a parable interpreted by Jesus. Rules of interpreting parables can be learned from it.

5:6-8; Gal. 5:9; see also Gen. 19:3; Ex. 12:15).[4] Might Jesus have used the symbol of leaven in both ways, simultaneously, if the doctrine being illustrated called for it (e.g., at 16:6, 12)?

IV. FOR THOUGHT AND DISCUSSION

Many warnings, encouragements, and challenges appear in this passage. Make three such lists, and apply them to the world and the church today.

V. FURTHER STUDY

1. Relate this chapter to what Matthew has already recorded about the kingdom.
2. You may want to study the parables of Jesus in depth. Two recommended sources are G. Campbell Morgan, *The Parables and Metaphors of Our Lord* (Westwood, N.J.: Revell, 1943), and Herbert Lockyer, *All the Parables of the Bible* (Grand Rapids: Zondervan, 1963).

VI. WORDS TO PONDER

The shallow, rocky soil represents the heart of a man who hears the message and receives it with real joy, but he doesn't have much depth in his life, and the seeds don't root very deeply (13:20-21a; *The Living Bible*).

---

4. A concise study of the Bible references to leaven may be found in *The Zondervan Pictorial Bible Dictionary*, p. 481.

Mission of the King

The passage of this lesson is the fourth main narrative section of Matthew's gospel. It is the story of the Son of Man's performing His last ministries in the regions of Galilee before turning toward Jerusalem for the cross. It is a composite picture of the King's mission wrought with a heart of compassion for the lost and submission to His heavenly Father. You will learn many precious truths from this portion of Matthew's inspired account.

I. PREPARATION FOR STUDY

1. Since this passage is unusually long, you will want to study it in several units. For example, three study units could be 13:54–14:36; 15:1–16:12; 16:21–17:27.

CONTEXT OF 13:54—17:27   **Chart O**

1:1	4:12	16:21	28:20
PRESENTATION of the KING	PROCLAMATION of the KING	PASSION of the KING	

	13:1	13:54	17:27	18:1	19:1b
	DISCOURSE — PARABLES	NARRATIVE — MISSION of the KING		DISCOURSE — GREATNESS	

this lesson

65

2. Chart O shows the context of this lesson in Matthew. Review Chart D, noting the two key phrases "began to preach" (4:12) and "began to show" (16:21) at the two main junctures of the gospel account. Observe that the passage of this lesson includes events before and after the pivotal point of 16:21. Review the two contrasted lists (e.g., multitudes—disciples) shown on Chart D on each side of the vertical line at 16:21.

3. Review Chart B. Make a mental note that the passage of this lesson is dated from the end of the middle Galilean period to the closing weeks of the later Galilean period.

4. Read 16:21 and 17:23. Since Jesus knew at this time that He would soon be concluding His earthly mission, how might He have arranged to have the gospel preached after He was gone? Your answer to this question will partly explain why Jesus' disciples are referred to in all but one of the sixteen paragraphs of this section.

II. ANALYSIS

Segment to be analyzed: 13:54–17:27
Paragraph divisions: at verses 13:54; 14:1, 13, 22; 15:1, 12, 21, 29, 32; 16:1, 13, 21, 24; 17:1, 14, 24

A. General Analysis

Chart P is a work sheet for recording general observations in this passage. Begin by assigning a paragraph title to each paragraph (an example is given). This will give you an overall view of the section. Then make notations in the other columns whenever the subject shown in the heading is a part of a paragraph. After doing this, answer the question: What are your impressions of Jesus' mission at this point in His career?

B. Paragraph Analysis

1. *Paragraph 13:54-58*
What is the people's problem?

_____

_____

66

PARAGRAPH	TITLE	MIRACLES and their EFFECTS	OPPOSITION	MULTITUDES	DISCIPLES	JESUS' MISSION MISINTERPRETED
13:54-58	"his own country"	not many	—offense —unbelief			rejected as GOD-MAN
14:1-12						
13-21						
22-36						
15:1-11	BEGINNING OF THE LATER GALILEAN MINISTRY					
12-20						
21-28						
29-31						
32-39						
16:1-12						
13-20						
	"From that time forth began Jesus to shew unto his disciples" (16:21)					
21-23						
24-28						
17:1-13						
14-23						
24-27						

67

How is this represented in the key question, "Whence hath this man ... ?"

___

___

2. Paragraph 14:1-12
Verses 3-12 are a parenthesis here. Try reading 14:1-2 immediately followed by 14:13.
Compare the contexts of the three references to "heard."
(a) "At that time Herod ... heard" (14:1)
(b) "When Jesus heard" (14:13)
(c) "When the people had heard" (14:13)
What does this paragraph contribute to the story of Jesus' mission?

___

___

3. Paragraph 14:13-21
What things impress you about this story?

___

___

___

4. Paragraph 14:22-36
Observe the many contrasts of this paragraph.
What does verse 23 teach about prayer?

___

___

Does verse 33 support the view that people were given enough light through Jesus' ministry to recognize His deity?

___

___

5. Paragraph 15:1-11
This confrontation took place at the beginning of the later Galilean period (see Chart B). Where had the scribes and Pharisees come from (15:1)?

___

___

Observe the repeated words "tradition" and "commandment." What was Jesus' teaching about these two standards?

_____

_____

Focus your study on this progression:
    (a) "transgress the *tradition* of the elders" (15:2)
    (b) "transgress the *commandment* of God by your *tradition*" (15:3)
    (c) "Ye have made the *commandment* of God of none effect by your *tradition*" (15:6)
6. *Paragraph 15:12-20*
What parable does Peter refer to in verse 15? (See vv. 11, 17.)

_____

The phrases that are the key to the meaning of the parable are "goeth into" and "cometh out of" (15:11). How does Jesus apply the parable?

_____

_____

7. *Paragraph 15:21-28*
This story teaches both the particular and universal objects of Christ's mission.
    (a) particular—mission to the Jews (cf. 10:5-6)
    (b) universal—mission also to the Gentiles (all non-Jews)
Study what the passage has to say about both. (Note: read Mark 7:26, which identifies the woman as a Greek.)
8. *Paragraph 15:29-31*
What is significant about the last phrase of the paragraph, "And they glorified the God of Israel?"

_____

_____

9. *Paragraph 15:32-39*
Compare this miracle with the similar one of 14:13-21.

_____

_____

10. *Paragraph 16:1-12*
Review 12:38-40. What two groups does Jesus deal with in this paragraph?

_____

_____

How does He.address each group (v. 3 and v. 8)?

_____

_____

CHRIST'S IDENTITY IN HIS EARTHLY CAREER **Chart Q**

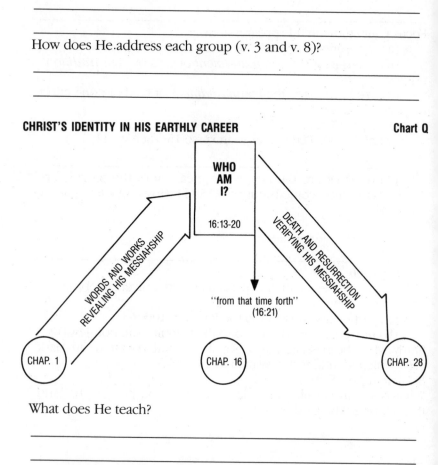

What does He teach?

_____

_____

11. *Paragraph 16:13-20*
This is a pivotal point in Jesus' public ministry. Chart Q shows the pattern.
How did Peter identify Christ (16:16)?

_____

_____

What was the source of his insight?

_____

_____

Explain verses 18 and 19.

_____

_____

Account for the prohibition of verse 20.

_____

_____

12. *Paragraph 16:21-23*
This is the first recorded instance of Jesus explicitly foretelling His coming death and resurrection. Can you recall an earlier occasion when He foretold it by Old Testament type or implied it?

_____

_____

How do you account for Peter's objection (v. 22)?

_____

_____

Explain Jesus' intentions in the words "Get thee behind me, Satan" (16:23).

_____

_____

13. *Paragraph 16:24-28*
What are the important lessons of discipleship taught here?

_____

_____

_____

What may verse 28 be a reference to?

_____

_____

14. *Paragraph 17:1-13*
Relate this event to 16:28. What are the important teachings of the paragraph?

_____

_____

_____

_____

What are your favorite statements of the text?

_____

_____

_____

15. *Paragraph 17:14-23*
What further lessons did the disciples learn from this experience?

_____

_____

16. *Paragraph 17:24-27*
Following the custom described in verses 25 and 26, in what sense was Jesus exempt from paying tax for the support of God's temple?

_____

_____

III. NOTES

1. *"Take the children's bread and cast it to dogs"* (15:26). Jews referred to themselves as children of God, and to Gentiles as dogs. The Greek word Jesus used, translated "dogs," is better translated "little dogs." These were the house pets, not the wild dogs that roamed the villages. So Jesus softened the metaphor, but He still told this Gentile "what He had told a Samaritan woman, that at this time all were dependent on Israel for Messiah and His blessings (John 4:21-23)."[1]

2. *"Upon this rock I will build my church"* (16:18). The phrase "this rock" has been figuratively interpreted in various ways, including the man Peter, his confession of faith, or Christ. If Peter is meant, it is "not Peter alone or mainly or primarily," because at

1. Homer A. Kent, "The Gospel According to Mark," in *The Wycliffe Bible Commentary*, p. 957.

the most, Peter was first among equals, by being the apostles' spokesman at this time and during the early years of the Acts period.[2]

3. *"The keys of the kingdom"* (16:19). Historically speaking, Peter was the servant who opened the door of the kingdom to believers for the first time when he preached his sermon on the day of Pentecost (Acts 2:14-40; cf. 8:14-17; 15:7).

4. *"Whatsoever thou shalt bind . . . loose"* (16:19). This authority was also given to all the disciples (18:18). Compare John 20:23, which is probably a reference to the same thing—remitting and retaining sins. No man can forgive sins (Mark 2:7).[3] But when a person proclaims the terms of salvation in Christ, he can assure his hearers that forgiveness of sins will be given by God if those terms are met. See NASB reading.

5. *"Get thee behind me, Satan"* (16:23). Peter meant well, but Satan was behind the words (cf. 4:10). It was the Father's plan to sacrifice His Son on the cross. Any attempt to thwart that plan was inspired by Satan.

6. *"The Son of man coming in his kingdom"* (16:28). Various interpretations of this "coming" include Christ's resurrection, the beginning of the church, and the destruction of Jerusalem (A.D. 70). The preferred view is that of the transfiguration of Christ, reported next in Matthew's account.

IV. FOR THOUGHT AND DISCUSSION

1. Was Jesus' ministry a success up to this point in Matthew's gospel? Justify your answer.

2. Is Jesus performing all the ministries in the world today that He did while on earth? Justify or illustrate your answer.

3. What have you learned about faith from this portion of Matthew?

4. What do you consider to be essential qualities of good Christian discipleship?

V. FURTHER STUDY

1. Consult various commentaries on the passage of Jesus' charge to Peter (16:13-20).

2. Read Romans 1:16; 2:9-10. Compare these verses with Matthew 10:5-6; 15:21-28 and Ephesians 2:11-18. How do these pas-

2. A. T. Robertson, *Word Pictures in the New Testament,* 1:132-34.
3. This is not to be confused with reconciliation between two persons when the offender repents and the offended one forgives him (e.g., Luke 17:3).

sages reveal God's schedule concerning proclaiming the gospel to Jews and Gentiles?

VI. WORDS TO PONDER

And when they had lifted up their eyes, they saw no man, save Jesus only (17:8).

Christians Living in Harmony

Not long after Jesus called the twelve disciples to himself, they began to be proud of their calling. And since pride begets jealousy and disunity, their effectiveness in teamwork was in jeopardy. This is why Jesus spent long hours with His close disciples counseling them about their personal spiritual problems, to make them vessels fit for His use. All Christians can profit much from the counsel of Jesus recorded in this chapter of Matthew.

I. PREPARATION FOR STUDY

Read Mark 9:33-35, which gives a few more details of the setting of this discourse than does the Matthew passage. How would you describe the feeling of the disciples toward each other at this time?

II. ANALYSIS

Segment to be analyzed: 18:1–1*a*
Paragraph divisions: at verses 1, 15, 21

A. General Analysis

1. Read the passage once, for overall impressions. Identify the three paragraphs by a common theme.

2. In this passage, how does Jesus teach about true greatness, as suggested earlier in this lesson?

B. Paragraph Analysis

1. *Paragraph 18:1-14*
What does Jesus use for His object lesson?

_____

_____

How many times is the word "little" repeated here?

_____

_____

Is Jesus teaching just about children literally, or does the word "children" represent certain kinds of people of all ages?

_____

_____

If the latter, cite an example.

_____

_____

Analyze this paragraph in three parts, suggested by the phrases listed below.

 a) "Become as little children" (18:3-4)
 b) "offend not these little ones" (18:5-9)
 c) "despise not these little ones" (18:10-14)

What do these three parts teach about the following: *true greatness* of man is measured in part by *his attitude* toward (a) those he thinks are inferior and (b) those who sin against him

2. *Paragraph 18:15-20*
What attitude of heart does Jesus appeal to here?

_____

_____

How much of this paragraph has *restoration* in view?

_____

_____

Jesus uses this opportunity to teach how the local Christian church should minister in restoring a sinner to its fellowship. What does He say about the church assembled (18:20)?

_____

_____

About the church praying (18:19)?

_____

_____

About the church's message and authority (18:17-18; cf. John 20:23)?

_____

_____

3. *Paragraph 18:21–19:1a*
Relate verse 21 to verse 15. What may have been Peter's thoughts when he asked, "Till seven times?" (See *Notes*.)

_____

What is the main point of this paragraph?

_____

Why would Jesus speak at length on this subject?

_____

What is the awesome pronouncement of verse 35?

_____

_____

III. NOTES

1. *"Their angels"* (18:10). God has appointed angels to minister in behalf of His people (Heb. 1:14; cf. Luke 1:19). Only eternity will reveal the full extent of these services.

2. *"Till seven times"* (18:21). Jews of Jesus' day were well acquainted with the rabbinical tradition of extending forgiveness not more than three times. Peter may have had this in mind when he suggested the generous seven forgivings. The idea of *entirety* as suggested by the symbolic number seven may also be involved here.

3. *"Ten thousand talents"* (18:24). Whatever their purchasing power, this large sum of money was 300,000 times the value of the hundred pence of verse 28.[1]

1. One hundred pence (one hundred denarii) represented the wages of one hundred days labor. Ten thousand talents were the equivalent of 30 million denarii.

IV. FOR THOUGHT AND DISCUSSION

Subjects suggested are:
1. genuine humility
2. restoration and reconciliation in Christian circles
3. disciplinary function of the local church
4. genuine forgiveness (cf. Matt. 18:35; Col. 3:13)
5. prayer petitions (cf. Matt. 18:19; 1 John 5:14)

V. FURTHER STUDY

Study the Bible's teaching about angels. Use a Bible dictionary or doctrine book for help in locating the Bible references.

VI. WORDS TO PONDER

Wherever two or three people come together in my name, I am there, **right among them!** (18:20, Phillips; emphasis added).

Lesson 12

19:1b–23:39

Final Ministries of the King

The next five chapters of Matthew report some of the final ministries of Jesus before His arrest. These were active days of teaching, preaching, and working miracles, as multitudes thronged about Jesus and Jewish leaders sought to destroy Him. The geographical setting includes the region of Perea, the city of Jerusalem, and the roads and villages in between.[1] (See the map, and have a mental picture of this geography as Matthew reports Jesus' movements.

I. PREPARATION FOR STUDY

1. You will probably want to study this passage in various units, because of its length. For example, three study units could be 19:1b–20:34; 21:1–22:14; 22:15–23:39. Or you could analyze the passage chapter by chapter, in five units.

2. Review Chart B and note where Matthew 19:1 is located, time-wise. Compare this location with that of 18:35 (originally written just previous to 19:1 without a chapter break). Thus Matthew reports little of the later Judean and Perean periods.[2]

3. Review Chart D as it relates to the passage of this lesson. Then study the accompanying Chart R, which shows the context of this lesson in the last major section of Matthew (16:21–28:20). What week of Jesus' life begins at 21:1?

---

1. The name Perea is not a New Testament word. It is a transliteration of the Greek *peran* ("beyond"), found in the phrase "beyond the Jordan" (Matt. 19:1). So Perea is the region opposite Judea on the eastern side of the Jordan River.
2. Luke and John are the main sources for these periods.

79

FURTHER TRAINING OF DISCIPLES		FINAL MINISTRIES		ARREST, TRIAL, DEATH, RESURRECTION, APPEARANCES	
16:21	19:1b	21:1	26:1	28:1	28:20
in Galilee	Perea, to Jerusalem	in Jerusalem			
	FEW DAYS	PASSION WEEK		DAY OF TRIUMPH	
		Sunday-Tuesday	24:1 Tuesday-Saturday	Sunday (and a later day)	
lesson →	this lesson (12)		13	14	15

II. ANALYSIS

Segment to be analyzed: 19:1b–23:39
Paragraph divisions: 19:1, 13, 16, 23; 20:1, 17, 20, 29; 21:1, 12, 18, 23, 33; 21:1, 15, 23, 34, 41; 23:1, 13, 34, 37

A. General Analysis

1. First mark the paragraph divisions in your Bible.
2. Then read the opening phrase of each paragraph. Make a mental note of people and places referred to here.
3. The work sheet of Chart S shows the different things to look for in this general study of the passage. Read the passage paragraph by paragraph, recording items as they appear in the Bible text. (An example is shown.) This exercise will give you a good grasp of the narrative.
4. Where in the passage does opposition persist paragraph after paragraph?

_____

_____

MATTHEW 19:1b—23:39

PARAGRAPH	GEOGRAPHY	MULTITUDES	DISCIPLES	OPPOSITION	SUBJECT OF DISCOURSE or CONVERSATION	MINISTRY
19:1-12	beyond Jordan			Pharisees	Divorce	—healing —instructing
13-15						
16-22						
23-30						
20:1-16						
17-19						
20-28						
29-34						
BEGINNING OF PASSION WEEK						
21:1-11						
12-17						
18-22						
23-27						
28-32						
33-46						
22:1-14						
15-22						
23-33						
34-40						
41-46						
23:1-12						
13-33						
34-36						
37-39						

5. Where is there a group of three parables?

_____

_____

6. What are your favorite passages in this lesson?

_____

_____

_____

B. Paragraph Analysis

1. *Paragraph 19:1b-12*
What does Jesus teach here about marriage?

_____

_____

about divorce?

_____

_____

2. *Paragraph 19:13-15*
What was the spiritual significance of Jesus' putting His hands on someone?

_____

_____

What does He teach about children in the few words of verse 14?

_____

_____

How old do you think these children were (cf. Mark 10:16)?
3. *Paragraph 19:16-22*
See an alternate reading of verses 16 and 17 in a modern version, such as NASB and *Berkeley*. What do you learn from the following statements of this conversation?
    (a) "What good thing shall I *do*, that I may *have* eternal life?"
    (b) "There is none good but one, that is, God."
    (c) "If thou wilt enter into life, keep the commandments."
    (d) "If thou wilt be perfect, go . . . sell . . . give . . . come . . . follow."
    (e) "He went away sorrowful."

4. *Paragraph 19:23-30*

How does the word "impossible" (v. 26) help to explain Jesus' illustration of the camel (v. 24)?

_____

How is Peter's statement "We have forsaken all" (c. 27) related to the two previous discussions about riches (19:20-22; 19:23-26)?

_____

What do you learn about Christian discipleship in verses 27-30?

_____

_____

5. *Paragraph 20:1-16*

How does 19:30 lead into this paragraph (compare 19:30 and 20:16)?

_____

What does Jesus teach about discipleship here?

_____

_____

_____

Explain "for many be called, but few chosen" (20:16).

_____

6. *Paragraph 20:17-19*

This short paragraph is one of the high peaks of Matthew. Compare the similar passage of 16:21-23. Could Jesus have prophesied His death and resurrection any more clearly?

Read Luke 24:4-12 and John 20:8-10 in light of this. How do you account for the no-impression effect of Jesus' prophecy?

_____

_____

7. Paragraph 20:20-28

James and John are the two sons involved here (Mark 10:35). Interpret and draw spiritual applications from the following verses.

v. 21

_____

v. 23*a*

_____

v. 23*b*

_____

What does this passage add to what Jesus had taught about true greatness in chapter 18?

_____

_____

Is Jesus being vain in citing Himself as an example of this kind of greatness (v. 28)?

_____

_____

Read "for many" (v. 28) as "in the place of many." How does this teach substitutionary atonement?

_____

_____

8. Paragraph 20:29-34

List the many things taught about Jesus in this paragraph. (There are more truths than appear at first sight.)

_____

_____

How is 20:28 fulfilled here?

_____

_____

9. Paragraph 21:1-11

Now begins the last week of Jesus' earthly career His death. This is called Passion Week. Chart T shows how the week proceeded for Jesus.[3]

3. For a detailed listing of all the events of this week, see *The Life of Christ* in this self-study series, pages 86-87.

KING EXTOLLED					KING MOCKED
MINISTRY TO PUBLIC			MINISTRY TO DISCIPLES		SOLITARY MINISTRY
SUNDAY	MONDAY	TUESDAY	WEDNESDAY	THURSDAY	FRIDAY
ACTIVE DAYS			QUIET DAYS		VIOLENT DAY
authority			compassion		submission
Jesus speaks much					Jesus speaks little

RIDING
INTO THE CITY
ON A COLT
(Matt. 21:1-11)

DRIVEN
OUT OF THE CITY
BEARING A CROSS
(John 19:17)

Jesus' entry into Jerusalem on Sunday has been called "The Triumphal Entry." What in this passage suggests triumph?

_____

_____

_____

What is the key question of verse 10?

_____

_____

How did the multitude answer it (v. 11)?

Do you think the "multitudes" of the procession (v. 9) and "multitude of verse 11 were two different groups or the same? Justify your answer.

_____

_____

_____

10. Paragraph 21:12-17

Matthew here groups together two different kinds of actions by Jesus and two contrasting reactions by people. What are they?

11. Paragraph 21:18-22

See *Notes* on the fig tree. What is taught about faith and prayer here?

12. Paragraph 21:23-27

What did the chief priests and elders challenge about Jesus?

What was their real problem?

13. Paragraphs 21:28–22:14

What is the main point of each parable? Record in your own words.
(a) 21:28-32

(b) 21:33-46

(c) 22:1-14

What does 21:45-46 reveal about Jesus' enemies?

about the perception of His mission?

14. Paragraphs 22:15–23:23

The remainder of this section of Matthew reports Jesus' confrontations with His opponents or words concerning them. Read the first sentence of each paragraph. Observe how the opponents initiate the conversation in the first three paragraphs and how Jesus takes the initiative in speaking in the remaining paragraphs. When were the opponents silenced, and what brought this about?

_____

_____

As you read each paragraph, record observations on the work sheet of Chart U. After you have completed this, make a list of the various teachings of Jesus that arose out of these confrontations.

_____

Answer the following questions about each paragraph.
(a) 22:15-22. Were the statements of verse 16 made in honesty (see v. 18)?

_____

(b) 22:23-33. What problem of the Sadducees does Jesus deal with in verses 31-32?

_____

_____

What is the impact of the words "that which was spoken unto you" (22:31).

_____

_____

c) 22:34-40. Explain verse 40.

_____

_____

Does this apply to today? If so, illustrate.

_____

_____

d) 22:41-46. Observe the key question, "What think ye of Christ?" Why was it not enough for the Pharisees to grant that Jesus was of the lineage of David?

_____

_____

JESUS AND THE OPPOSITION
22:15—23:39

OPPONENTS CHALLENGE JESUS

PARAGRAPH	OPPONENTS	THEIR CHALLENGE	JESUS' REPLY	EFFECT
22:15-22				
23-33				
34-40				

JESUS CHARGES HIS OPPONENTS

PARAGRAPH	OPPONENTS INVOLVED	JESUS' CHARGE	JESUS' TEACHING	EFFECT
22:41-46				
23:1-12				
13-33				
34-36				
37-39				

Compare 20:30-31; 21:9, 15-16.
(e) 23:1-12. What sins does Jesus expose here?

_____

_____

_____

(f) 23:13-33. What is the repeated phrase?

_____

_____

How is it a clue to the main point of Jesus' strong charges?

_____

Make a list of the charges, in your own words.

_____

_____

(g) 23:34-36. What is the tone of this paragraph?

_____

_____

What sin did Jesus prophesy that His hearers would commit?

_____

Was the prophecy fulfilled before the end of New Testament times?

_____

(h) 23:37-39. What is the underlying tone of these words of Jesus?

_____

What does this reveal about Him?

_____

_____

Is the first half of verse 39 being fulfilled today in Israel's history?

_____

When will the last half of verse 39 take place? (Read Romans 11 and Zechariah 12:10.)

_____

_____

How is this paragraph a natural conclusion to this section of Matthew's gospel?

III. NOTES

1. *"A rich man shall hardly enter into the kingdom of heaven"* (19:23). This is better translated, "It is hard for a rich man to enter the kingdom of heaven" (NASB). The difficulty had just been demonstrated in verse 22.

2. *"In the regeneration"* (19:28). Merrill F. Unger writes, "This regeneration . . . refers to the renewal of the earth in the mediatorial Davidic kingdom offered and rejected (Matt. 3-12) but restored at the second advent (Matt. 25:31). This kingdom will evidently be administered over Israel by the 12 apostles (cf. Isa. 1:26)."[4]

3. *"Shall deliver him to the Gentiles"* (20:19). The crime of which Jesus was eventually accused by the Jews—blasphemy— was of a theological nature, so the case was tried before Jewish authorities (20:18). The court gave the death sentence; but since only the Roman civil powers could carry out such a sentence, Jesus was referred to the Roman rulers, Pilate and Herod, for execution.

4. *"Cup . . . baptism"* (20:22-23). Both references are to Christ's sufferings, including His death (cf. 26:39). Most if not all of the apostles shared in the fate of suffering and death as martyrs. But none of them could die as He died—as a substitutionary atonement for the sins of men.

5. *"Hosanna"* (21:9). This Hebrew word means "save, now" or "save, Lord." Compare Psalm 118:25-26; 2 Samuel 14:4. In time the word came to be used more as praise to the Saviour than as a plea for salvation.

6. *"Let no fruit grow on thee hence forward"* (21:19). This was a parable in action. There should have been figs on the tree with the crop of leaves, since the early figs in the spring began appearing before the leaves. The lesson of pretension and false profession is clear.

7. *"As the angels of God in heaven"* (22:30). The comparison here is only in the matter of marriage.

8. *"From the blood of righteous Abel unto the blood of Zacharias"* (23:35). Jesus here is including all such murders of Old Tes-

4. Merrill F. Unger, *Unger's Bible Handbook*, p. 483.

tament times by citing the first one recorded in Scripture, that of Abel (Gen. 4:8), and the last, that of Zacharias (2 Chron. 24:20-22). (In the Hebrew canon 2 Chronicles is the last book to be listed.)[5]

IV. FOR THOUGHT AND DISCUSSION

Think more about what the Bible teaches about the following.

1. *Material wealth*. "The difficulty with wealth lies not in its possession (many righteous men in Scripture had wealth—Abraham, Job, Joseph of Arimathea) but in the false trust it inspires (1 Tim. 6:17; Mark 10:24)."[6]

2. *Obligations to our government*. Compare 22:21 with such passages as Romans 13:1-7; 1 Peter 2:13-16; Acts 4:19-20.

3. *Life in heaven*. Compare 22:29-30 with 1 Corinthians 15:40-50. What will life in heaven be like, as far as each believer's individual experience is concerned? Will our identities be lost?

4. *Hypocrisy*. What do you think about hypocrisy in Christian circles?

V. FURTHER STUDY

Study other references in the New Testament to the subjects of marriage and divorce.

VI. WORDS TO PONDER

O Jerusalem, Jerusalem ... How often I have wanted to gather your children together ... **but you wouldn't let me** (23:37; *The Living Bible*, emphasis added).

5. The Jewish and Protestant Old Testaments are the same in content but differ in the listed order and combinations of books.
6. Homer A. Kent, in *The Wycliffe Bible Commentary*, p. 964.

Lesson 13

The King's Second Coming

The last discourse of Jesus recorded in Matthew is a prophecy of His second coming to earth. The concluding verse of chapter 23 studied in the last lesson reports Jesus foretelling briefly that distant advent and relating it especially to the Jews He was addressing. Though the extended discourse that follows (24:1–26:1) is addressed to His disciples, one might say that these prophecies are Jesus' farewell message to Israel through His disciples in the role of representative Israelites.[1] So the prophecies known as the Olivet Discourse[2] are a natural follow-up of Jesus' confrontations with Jewish leaders who were plotting His death. Here are Christ's descriptions of the end of this age prior to establishing His kingdom on earth, *especially as it relates to Israel and Israel's program.* As we shall observe in our studies, much tribulation awaits Israel for rejecting their Messiah, though a remnant of believers will be delivered.

I. INTRODUCTORY REMARKS

Some preliminary observations are in order before the Bible text is analyzed in detail.

1. The Olivet Discourse is reported by all three synoptic gospels: Matthew 24-25; Mark 13; Luke 21. Matthew gives the longest coverage, which is partly explained by the fact that Matthew wrote especially for Jews and the Olivet Discourse involved Israel primarily.

---

1. See Merrill F. Unger, *Unger's Bible Dictionary* (Chicago: Moody, 1957), p. 808.
2. So named because Jesus and His disciples were on the Mount of Olives at this time. The panorama of Jerusalem and its Temple from this spot was beautiful and awe-inspiring (Mark. 13:1).

2. The predictive parts of this passage pose the same kinds of difficulties that attend most Bible prophecies of end times. This is God's clue to us to be cautious about our interpretations and to place most weight on the parts that are clear.

3. For some reason, Matthew and Mark do not report the explicit prophecy of Jerusalem's fall, as Luke does. Read Luke 21:20-24. In verse 24 Jesus prophesied that Jerusalem would be conquered by non-Jews[3] (fulfilled in A.D. 70); this to be followed by an era of opportunity for the Gentile world; then Israel's final restoration to favor (cf. Rom. 11:25-27; Isa. 2:3; Jer. 31; Zech. 14:4). Current events are now writing some of the concluding fulfillments to this prophecy.

4. How you interpret this discourse is determined largely by how you view prophecies of the Bible concerning the Millennium. Chart V shows the course of Israel's history in the premillennial scheme of world events. Read Acts 1:6-8, and observe that just before Jesus' ascension to heaven the disciples were still asking when the kingdom would be restored.[4] Jesus' answer did not deny the fact of a restored kingdom. What did He correct, however? It may be observed here that premillennialists view the millennial kingdom on earth as a fulfillment of Old Testament promises preeminently to Israel as a nation. The zenith of Christ's glorious reign will be in heaven for eternity.

5. The key event on Chart V is Christ's second coming to the earth. It is also the key event of the Olivet Discourse. Read Matthew 24:3, 27, 30, 37, 39, 42, 44, 46; 25:13, 31. In the Olivet Discourse this coming of Christ is not the *rapture* phase, when He shall come only to the clouds (1 Thess. 4:14-17). Rather, it is the *revelation* phase, when He shall come to earth.[5]

II. ANALYSIS

Segment to be analyzed: 24:1–25:36
Paragraph divisions: at verses 24:1, 9, 15, 23, 29, 32, 36, 42, 45; 25:1, 14, 31

---

3. The words "nations" and "Gentiles" in Luke 21:24 translate the same Greek word.
4. The story of Israel's kingdom in Old Testament times was tragedy. The promised messianic kingdom was to be a glorious, miraculous restoration.
5. These descriptions represent the pretribulation view of premillennialism.

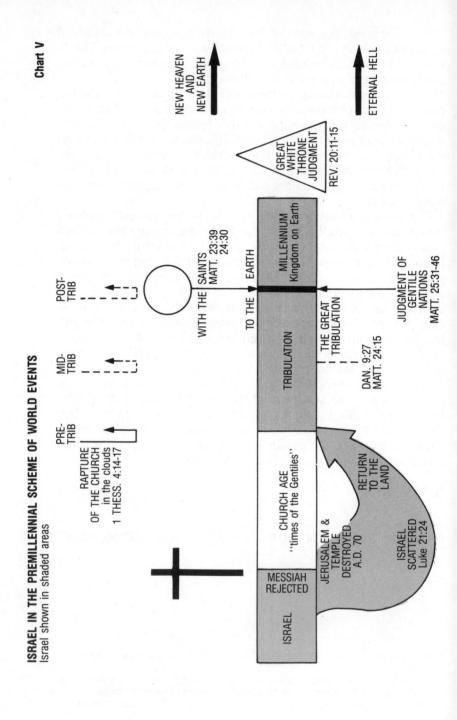

ISRAEL IN THE PREMILLENNIAL SCHEME OF WORLD EVENTS
Israel shown in shaded areas

Chart V

NEW HEAVEN AND NEW EARTH

ETERNAL HELL

GREAT WHITE THRONE JUDGMENT
REV. 20:11-15

MILLENNIUM
Kingdom on Earth

WITH THE SAINTS
MATT. 23:39
24:30

TO THE EARTH

JUDGMENT OF GENTILE NATIONS
MATT. 25:31-46

POST-TRIB

MID-TRIB

PRE-TRIB

RAPTURE OF THE CHURCH
in the clouds
1 THESS. 4:14-17

TRIBULATION

THE GREAT TRIBULATION

DAN. 9:27
MATT. 24:15

CHURCH AGE
"times of the Gentiles"

MESSIAH REJECTED

ISRAEL

JERUSALEM & TEMPLE DESTROYED A.D. 70

RETURN TO THE LAND

ISRAEL SCATTERED
Luke 21:24

94

A. General Analysis

Some suggestions for study are given below. Let these be starters for more detailed studies. Most of the suggestions concern the highlights of the discourse.

1. First mark the foregoing paragraph divisions in your Bible. Then read the entire passage for overall impressions. What do you observe about quantity of the following:
(a) detailed events:

_____

(b) exhortations and warnings:

_____

(c) parables

_____

2. What three questions did the disciples ask Jesus (24:3)?

_____

_____

_____

Did Jesus answer all three?

_____

3. Did Jesus include calendar dates in His prophecies?

_____

Observe references to time in the following verses.
24:3

_____

24:6

_____

24:8-9

_____

24:13

_____

24:14

_____

24:15

_____

24:29-30

25:31

SIX SECTIONS OF THE OLIVET DISCOURSE   Chart W
(24:4—25:46)

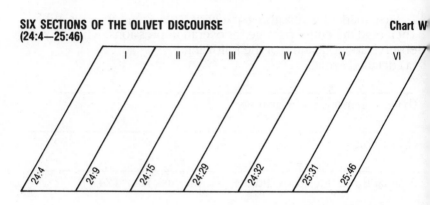

4. Chart W shows the six main sections of the Matthew passage. Scan the entire passage once again and try to account for the dividing points. Record in the blank spaces the main content of each section. Which section is more practical exhortation than it is detailed prophecy?

5. One of the clear features of this discourse is the chronological progression of events. Read the passage again, observing where each event or period appears on Chart X. Record a general description of the two periods shown.

B. Paragraph Analysis

1. *Paragraphs 24:4-8; 9-14; 15-22*
Study the three paragraphs in connection with Charts V and X. Compare the prophecies of Matthew 24:4-14 and the seals of Revelation 6. Read Daniel 9:27; 11:31 for background to Matthew 24:15. Refer to commentaries for help on this. Try to reach some conclusions as to when the events and periods of Chart X, before Christ's coming, will transpire (for example, whether during the church age or during Great Tribulation in the end times). This will be your most difficult task. Where you place 24:14 and 24:15 in the order of world events will determine to a great extent the

remainder of your conclusions.[6] Note where 24:15 is placed on Chart V.[7] What description of tribulation in 24:21-22 tells you that those times are *end times*. (See *Further Study*, which shows five different interpretations of this section. This diversity of views confirms the difficulty of the passage.)

RONOLOGICAL PROGRESSION OF OLIVET DISCOURSE   **Chart X**

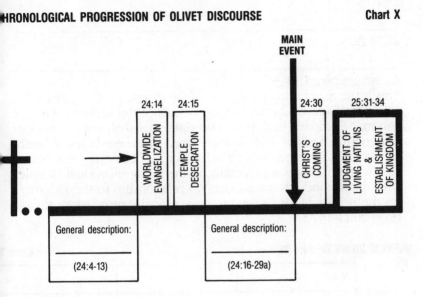

2. *Paragraphs 24:23-28, 29-31*
What do you learn from these paragraphs about Christ's coming?

_____

_____

3. *Paragraphs 24:32-35; 36-41; 42-44; 45-51; 25:1-13; 14-30*
From a practical standpoint, this is the most important section of the discourse. Record the main teachings of the paragraphs listed below.
24:32-35

_____

24:36-41

_____

6. Kent locates 24:14 in the Tribulation, holding that the gospel will be preached "through the efforts of the two witnesses (Rev. 11:3-12) and the sealed remnant of Israel (Rev. 7)" (*Wycliffe Bible Commentary*, p. 972).
7. See ibid.

24:42-44

24:45-51

25:1-13

25:14-30

4. Paragraph 25:31-36

This is the concluding paragraph of the discourse. The phrase "all nations" of verse 32 refers to individuals of the surviving Gentile nations.[8] Compare Joel 3:1-2. The righteous shall enter the kingdom on the basis of their faith-activated treatment of Jesus' brethren (25:40), here probably a reference to believing Jews. Pentecost writes, "This is a judgment on the living individual Gentiles after the second advent and has no relationship to the judgment on the *dead* who are raised to appear at the great white throne (Rev. 20:11-15)"[9]

VARIOUS VIEWS OF 24:4-28   **Chart Y**

	24:4	24:9	24:15	24:28
1	present church age		Great Tribulation	
2	present age	Tribulation		
3	present age and Tribulation (double perspective)			
4	first half of Tribulation		last half of Tribulation	
5	first half of Tribulation	last half of Tribulation		

8. The same Greek word is translated "nations" and "Gentiles." See *Berkeley Version*, footnote.
9. J. Dwight Pentecost, *Things to Come*, p. 284.

III. NOTES

As mentioned earlier, you probably will want to refer to commentaries for help on the difficult portions of this passage. First, however, you should complete a fair amount of independent study, looking especially for the things that are clear.

IV. FOR THOUGHT AND DISCUSSION

How can you as a Christian apply the Olivet Discourse to your life today? For example, are the spiritual lessons of the parables applicable to the imminent rapture of the church, even though this event may not be part of the prophecy?

V. FURTHER STUDY

Chart Y shows five different interpretations of 24:4-28 by premillennialists. Try to determine how each view was derived from the Bible text.[10]

VI. WORDS TO PONDER

Watch therefore, for ye know neither the day nor the hour wherein the Son of man cometh (25:13).

---

10. Views shown on the chart are essentially those held by the following: (1) W. Graham Scroggie; (2) Lewis S. Chafer; (3) C.I. Scofield; (4) E. Schuyler English; (5) J. Dwight Pentecost. See J. Dwight Pentecost, *Things to Come*, pp. 275ff.

Lesson 14

Death and Burial of the King

Jesus not only prophesied His death and resurrection, but He also knew the exact days of their fulfillment. This is the sure note on which Matthew opens his account of the final days of Jesus leading to Calvary. The remainder of the passage is wave after wave of deep and tender pathos. Only the hardened soul can read this story without becoming emotionally involved.

I. PREPARATION FOR STUDY

Read Exodus 12, which describes the origin of Israel's Passover memorial. What did the Passover typify in Old Testament days? How significant was it that Jesus was slain on the very holiday that pointed to Him (cf. Matt. 26:2)?

II. ANALYSIS

Segment to be analyzed: 26:1–27:66
Paragraph divisions: at verses 26:1, 6, 14, 17, 26, 31, 36, 47, 57, 69; 27:1, 3, 11, 27, 32, 45, 57, 62

A. General Analysis

First read the passage paragraph by paragraph for major impressions. Record paragraph titles on Chart Z. (Examples are shown.) This will help you get an overall view of Jesus' experiences during these days. Note on the chart that the passage reports events of three days of Passion Week. (We observe the Wednesday "silence" in an earlier lesson.)

Study the outline on the chart. You may want to add an outline of your own.

100

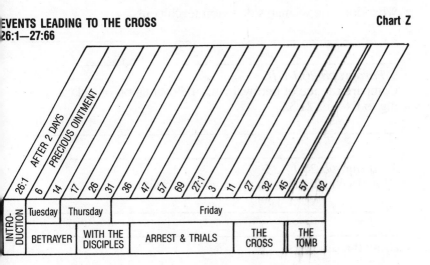

B. Paragraph Analysis

In addition to answering the questions given below, study each paragraph for its presentation of Jesus as: Prophet, Priest, King, Sacrifice, Son of Man, Son of God.

1. *Paragraph 26:1-5*
How is this an introduction to the story?

_____

_____

Compare Jesus' prophecy about time (26:2) and the rulers' preference (26:5).

_____

_____

_____

2. *Paragraph 26:6-13*
This is a parenthesis in Matthew's story. Here he is recalling what had transpired earlier (read John 12:1-8), showing how Judas and the other disciples at that time felt about the woman's act of devotion.[1] Matthew inserts the story here partly as background to the account of Judas in the next paragraph (26:14-16).

_____

1. John 12:4 identifies Judas by name.

What does the woman's devotion teach you?

_____

_____

3. *Paragraph 26:14-16*
Compare the fee of betrayal with the evaluation of a slave according to Exodus 21:32.

_____

_____

4. *Paragraph 26:17-25*
What do you learn from these verses about Jesus?

_____

about the disciples?

_____

about Judas?

_____

5. *Paragraphs 26:26-30; 31-35; 36-46*
How Jesus was preparing His disciples for His coming death is the common subject of these three paragraphs.
What kind of help and instruction did He give?

_____

_____

What are the various references to His death here?

_____

_____

6. *Paragraphs 26:47-56; 57-68; 69-75; 27:1-2; 3-10; 11-26*
Study these paragraphs under the heading on Chart Z. Look especially for the following.
    (a) Words of Jesus
    (b) Charges against Jesus
    (c) What influenced the multitudes to reject Jesus
    (d) The grief of one who denied Christ
    (e) The utter despair of one who betrayed Christ
7. *Paragraph 27:27-56*
The story of Jesus' crucifixion is the most moving story ever written. Studying such a passage as this need not be a coldhearted, objective analysis. In fact, Bible study that is Christian should involve the Christian's very heart, soul, and body—all of him. Ask the Holy

Spirit to open your eyes to see what He would have you see in this stirring record of the Calvary event.

8. *Paragraph 27:27-31*
What is the tone here?

_____

_____

Observe the various acts of mockery
9. *Paragraph 27:32-44*
How many words are used here to report the actual crucifixion?

_____

How do you explain such brevity?

_____

_____

Read Isaiah 52:13–53:12. How is this prophecy fulfilled here?

_____

_____

10. *Paragraph 27:45-56*
Read Psalm 22. How does the psalm reveal the thoughts of Jesus while He was hanging on the cross?

_____

_____

What verse in the Matthew passage records the moment of Christ's death?

_____

_____

What miraculous signs attended that death?

_____

_____

_____

What did each one symbolize?

_____

_____

_____

11. *Paragraphs 27:57-61; 27:62-66*
Compare the contents of both paragraphs. What is the tone of each?

_____

_____

Compare verse 61 and verse 66.

_____

_____

Recall the first two paragraphs of this passage: plot against Jesus (26:1-5) and devotion to Jesus (26:6-13). Compare these with the last two paragraphs of chapter 27.

_____

_____

III. FOR THOUGHT AND DISCUSSION

1. What have you learned from these chapters about the following?
(a) The love of Christ

_____

(b) Unbelief

_____

(c) The awfulness of sin

_____

(d) The power of God

_____

(e) The necessity of Christ's death on the cross

_____

_____

2. Reflect on the truth of this comment: "Today we are judged by the cross of Christ; and when we pass our verdict upon it, that is its verdict upon us."
3. What spiritual lessons can be learned from the stories here of the following?
(a) The woman with the alabaster box

_____

(b) Peter

_____

(c) The two Marys

_____

(d) Joseph of Arimathea

_____

4. What deep impressions do these chapters leave with you?

IV. FURTHER STUDY

Some subjects for extended study are suggested below.
    1. Descriptions of scourging (27:26) and crucifixion. Consult a Bible dictionary for this.
    2. The "seven last words" of Jesus on the cross.
        (a) Spoken from 9:00 A.M.–12:00 M.

        Luke 23:34   _____

        Luke 23:43   _____

        John 19:26   _____
        (b) Spoken from 12:00 M.–3:00 P.M.

        Matthew 27:46   _____

        John 19:28   _____

        John 19:30   _____

        Luke 23:46   _____

V. WORDS TO PONDER

My God, my God, why hast thou forsaken me? (27:46).

He whose very life was love, who thirsted for love as the hart pants for the waterbrooks, was encircled with a sea of hatred and of dark, bitter, hellish passion, that surged round Him and flung up its waves about His cross. His soul was spotlessly pure ... but sin pressed itself against it, endeavoring to force upon it its loathsome contact, from which it shrank through every fiber.[2]

2. James Stalker, _The Life of Jesus Christ_, p. 144.

Resurrection and Great Commission of the King

"If Christ be not risen, then is our preaching vain, and your faith is also vain."

So wrote Paul to the young converts of the church at Corinth (1 Cor. 15:14). The literal resurrection of the body of Jesus from the tomb of Golgotha is the cardinal fact of Christianity. There can be no Easter *faith* without the Easter *fact*. All four gospels make clear that Jesus was literally resurrected from the grave. The angel's announcement "He is not here: for he is risen" (Matt. 28:6) was as world shaking as it was brief. This resurrection chapter of Matthew gives meaning to the event of Calvary—and to all the facts of Jesus' life. As you study this lesson it should not be difficult for you to see that the resurrection was the supreme authentication of the kingship of Jesus. Only the King of kings could say truly, "All authority is given unto me in heaven and in earth" (Matt. 28:18).

I. PREPARATION FOR STUDY

1. Read Matthew 27:62-66 again, and observe the extra precautions taken by Jesus' enemies to prevent His body from being stolen. In what way is this strong support for the factuality of the empty-tomb narrative?

2. Jesus spent forty days in His resurrection body on this earth before He ascended to heaven (Acts 1:3). Chart AA shows generally where He spent those days. Note that Matthew 28 covers two parts of that period.

3. Ponder the uniqueness of Christianity among the religions of the world in its claim of a living Saviour who has been resurrected from the grave.

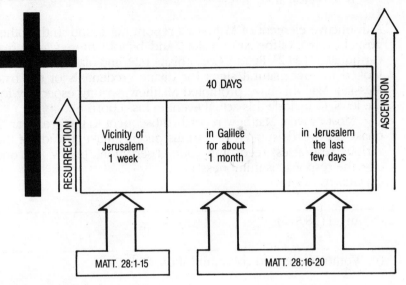

II. ANALYSIS

Segment to be analyzed: 28:1-20
Paragraph divisions: at verses 1, 9, 11, 16

A. General Analysis

1. Read the chapter, paragraph by paragraph. Record the main theme of each.
28:1-8

_____

28:9-10

_____

28:11-15

_____

28:16-20

_____

2. What items of this story are miraculous? List them one by one as they appear in the chapter.

B. A Topical Study

A distinctive element of Matthew's report, not found in the other gospels, is that of the earthquake. "And, behold, there was a great earthquake" (28:2). Read 1 Corinthians 1:22, and observe that Jews looked to supernatural signs for divine credentials of the true Messiah. May this have prompted Matthew, writing especially for the Jews, to include this actual event in his report?

Most of what Matthew records subsequent to the great earthquake are words spoken by various people. Make a study of the various responses, recording your observations below. (In one case the response is numbness!)

(a) Guards (28:4)

(b) Angel (28:5-7)

(c) Women (intended communication, 28:8-9)

(d) Jesus (28:9-10)

(e) Guards (28:11)

(f) Priests and elders (28:12-14)

(g) Eleven disciples (28:17)

(h) Jesus (28:18-20)

C. The Great Commission (28:18-20)

Jesus' commission to the disciples (28:18-20) is the bright conclusion of Matthew's gospel. It ties the gospel story to *today*. No Christian can evade its claims and promises. Spend time analyzing each word and phrase, applying the truths to your own life.

Observe among other things the four times "all" is repeated in the commission. The following outline is based on such an observation.[1]

1. Outline is from W.H. Griffith Thomas, *Outline Studies in the Gospel of Matthew* (Grand Rapids: Eerdmans, 1961), pp. 464-68.

1. The Secret of Service—"all authority" (v. 18)[2]
2. The Scope of Service—"all the nations" (v. 19)
3. The Substance of Service—"teaching . . . all things" (v. 20)
4. The Strength of Service—"I am with you all the days" (v. 20, lit.)

Conclusion

Matthew's gospel narrative begins with the story of Jesus' birth and concludes with His great commission, spoken thirty-three years later. In the advent story, wise men ask, "Where is he that is born King of the Jews?" (2:2). In the commissioning, the King commands, "Go ye therefore, and teach all nations" (28:19). As you complete your study of this gospel, try to recall the highlights of Jesus' ministry between that question and the command. Then ask yourself, "Have I really crowned Jesus as King of my life —Lord of all?"

---

2. The word translated "power" in 28:18 means power of authority, or right to exercise power.

A CHRONOLOGICAL ORDER OF
THE WRITING OF THE NEW TESTAMENT BOOKS

BOOK	AUTHOR		PLACE WRITTEN	DATE A.D.	PERIODS		
					Personnel	Apostolic Literature	Church
James	– James		Jerusalem	45		BEGINNINGS	FOUNDING
Galatians	Paul	JOURNEY EPISTLES		48	FIRST PAULINE PERIOD	BEGINNINGS	FOUNDING
1 Thessalonians	Paul	JOURNEY EPISTLES	Corinth	52	FIRST PAULINE PERIOD	BEGINNINGS	FOUNDING
2 Thessalonians	Paul	JOURNEY EPISTLES			FIRST PAULINE PERIOD	BEGINNINGS	FOUNDING
1 Corinthians	Paul	JOURNEY EPISTLES	Ephesus	55	FIRST PAULINE PERIOD	BEGINNINGS	FOUNDING
2 Corinthians	Paul	JOURNEY EPISTLES	Macedonia		FIRST PAULINE PERIOD	BEGINNINGS	FOUNDING
Romans	Paul	JOURNEY EPISTLES	Corinth	56	FIRST PAULINE PERIOD	BEGINNINGS	FOUNDING
Matthew	– Matthew		Jerusalem?	58	FIRST HISTORICAL RECORDS	BEGINNINGS	FOUNDING
Luke	Luke		Rome		FIRST HISTORICAL RECORDS	BEGINNINGS	FOUNDING
Acts	Luke		Rome	61	FIRST HISTORICAL RECORDS	BEGINNINGS	FOUNDING
Colossians	Paul	PRISON EPISTLES	Rome	61	CENTRAL PAULINE PERIOD	CENTRAL	ESTABLISHING
Ephesians	Paul	PRISON EPISTLES	Rome	61	CENTRAL PAULINE PERIOD	CENTRAL	ESTABLISHING
Philemon	Paul	PRISON EPISTLES	Rome	61	CENTRAL PAULINE PERIOD	CENTRAL	ESTABLISHING
Philippians	Paul	PRISON EPISTLES	Rome	61	CENTRAL PAULINE PERIOD	CENTRAL	ESTABLISHING
1 Timothy	Paul	PASTORAL EPISTLES	Macedonia	62	PAUL'S LEGACY	CENTRAL	ESTABLISHING
Titus	Paul	PASTORAL EPISTLES	Corinth?		PAUL'S LEGACY	CENTRAL	ESTABLISHING
2 Timothy	Paul	PASTORAL EPISTLES	Rome	67	PAUL'S LEGACY	CENTRAL	ESTABLISHING
Hebrews	– ?					CENTRAL	ESTABLISHING
Jude	– Jude					CENTRAL	ESTABLISHING
1 Peter	Peter				PETER'S LEGACY	CENTRAL	ESTABLISHING
2 Peter	Peter			68?	PETER'S LEGACY	CENTRAL	ESTABLISHING
Mark	– Mark				PETER'S LEGACY	CENTRAL	ESTABLISHING
John	John		Ephesus?	85	JOHN'S LEGACY	CLOSING	CONTINUING
1 John	John				JOHN'S LEGACY	CLOSING	CONTINUING
2 John	John				JOHN'S LEGACY	CLOSING	CONTINUING
3 John	John				JOHN'S LEGACY	CLOSING	CONTINUING
Revelation	John		Patmos	96	JOHN'S LEGACY	CLOSING	CONTINUING

Bibliography

SELECTED SOURCES FOR FURTHER STUDY

COMMENTARIES

Atkinson, B. F. C. "The Gospel According to Matthew," in *The New Bible Commentary*, ed. F. Davidson. Grand Rapids: Eerdmans, 1953.

Dunnett, Walter M. *An Outline of New Testament Survey*. Chicago: Moody, 1960.

Kent, Homer A. "The Gospel According to Matthew," in *The Wycliffe Bible Commentary*, ed. Charles F. Pfeiffer and Everett F. Harrison. Chicago: Moody, 1962.

Macauley, J. C. *Behold Your King*. Chicago: Moody, 1982.

Morgan, G. Campbell. *The Gospel According to Matthew*. Westwood, N.J.: Revell, 1929.

Scroggie, W. Graham. *Know Your Bible*. Vol. 2. Westwood, N.J.: Revell, 1965.

Walvoord, John F. *Thy Kingdom Come*. Chicago: Moody, 1974.

OTHER SOURCES

Jensen, Irving L. *Independent Bible Study*. Chicago: Moody, 1963.

————. *Jensen's Survey of the New Testament*. Chicago: Moody, 1981.

————. *The Life of Christ*. Chicago: Moody, 1969.

Pentecost, J. Dwight. *Things to Come*. Grand Rapids: Dunham, 1964.

Robertson, A. T. *A Harmony of the Gospels for Students of the Life of Christ*. Nashville: Broadman, 1922.

_____. *Word Pictures in the New Testament*. Vol. 1. New York: Harper, 1930.

Scroggie, W. Graham. *A Guide to the Gospels*. London: Pickering & Inglis, 1948.

Stalker, James. *The Life of Jesus Christ*. Westwood, N.J.: Revell, 1880.

Tenney, Merrill C. *The Zondervan Pictorial Bible Dictionary*. Grand Rapids: Zondervan, 1963.

Unger, Merrill F. *Unger's Bible Dictionary*. Chicago: Moody, 1957.

_____. *Unger's Bible Handbook*. Chicago: Moody, 1966.

Vine, W. E. *An Expository Dictionary of New Testament Words*. Westwood, N.J.: Revell, 1961.

Walvoord, John F. *Matthew*. Chicago: Moody, 1974.

Moody Press, a ministry of the Moody Bible Institute,
is designed for education, evangelization, and edification.
If we may assist you in knowing more about Christ
and the Christian life, please write us without obligation:
Moody Press, c/o MLM, Chicago, Illinois 60610.